The Mystery
of the Woman

ESSAYS ON THE MOTHER OF GOD
SPONSORED BY THE
DEPARTMENT OF THEOLOGY
UNIVERSITY OF NOTRE DAME

EDITED BY EDWARD D. O'CONNOR, C.S.C.

University of Notre Dame Press · Notre Dame, Indiana

IMPRIMI POTEST: Theodore J. Mehling, C.S.C.
Provincial

NIHIL OBSTAT: Albert L. Schlitzer, C.S.C.
Censor Deputatus

IMPRIMATUR: ✠ Leo A. Pursley, D.D., L.L.D.
Apostolic Administrator
Diocese of Fort Wayne

January 13, 1956

TO

HER OF WHOM THESE PAGES SPEAK

IN GRATITUDE

FOR THE PROTECTION AND INSPIRATION

OF HER CONSTANT PRESENCE

IN THE

UNIVERSITY OF NOTRE DAME

Illustrations by Peter Stavroulakis

For permission to use the frontispiece, acknowledgment is gratefully made to Fides Publishers' Association, Chicago, which has copyright to the woodcut, and to Father Luke Malik, O. P., owner of the original colored version.

CONTENTS

INTRODUCTION

When Pius XII proclaimed 1954 a Marian Year, all Catholic institutions dreamed of making some special contribution to the honor of Mary. The University of Notre Dame was under a particular compulsion of love and gratitude. Our University is named after Our Lady and dedicated to her. We have experienced daily the beneficent care which seems to flow like a special benediction from the Lady on the Golden Dome of Notre Dame.

Moreover, we are an American university whose growth and progress has, for over a century, paralleled that of our beloved country, long ago dedicated to Mary.

For these reasons, we planned this special volume. Its primary intent is to introduce Our Lady to fellow Americans not of our faith in a way that might give them some insight into Mary's place in our Catholic life. The initial approach is intellectual and theological, as befits a university.

Our theme is at once simple and profound. We have taken as our basic text the ancient antiphon used in the liturgy of the Virgin Mary: "Rejoice, O Virgin Mary, Thou alone hast destroyed all heresies." To illustrate this text, we have selected three of the key beliefs of Catholics regarding Mary: that she is the Mother of God; that she was conceived without original sin; and that at the end of her life she was assumed bodily into heaven. However, it is not our intention here to attempt to justify the Catholic faith about Mary. This has been done competently elsewhere. These pages seek to do no more than explain precisely what our beliefs are, and point out the deeper significance—perhaps sometimes unsuspected—that attaches to them.

All of these beliefs have been defined by the Church as the official faith of Catholics, and each represents an historical landmark in the positive answer of Faith to heresy.

The first doctrine, of the divine maternity, was defined at the Council of Ephesus in the year 431. It was the definitive answer to four centuries of doubt and controversy about the key doctrine of Christianity: that Christ is true God and true man, that He is one person, eternally proceeding from God the Father, and, in time, conceived in His humanity by the Virgin Mary. That Mary is the Mother of God, means that Christ is true man, and true God, and one Person. This doctrine is the basis for all the honor given Mary by Catholics, for all we say of her is pale praise beside what God Himself has done for her: chosen her to be the Mother of Christ. "He Who is mighty has done great things for me, and holy is His name." (Luke 1:49)

The second doctrine, of the Immaculate Conception, defined by Pius IX in 1854, answered all the errors about the soul of man and his redemption that came during the centuries after the Reformation. When we say that Mary was conceived without original sin, we are saying that all other men are born deprived of divine life and needing redemption. We are clearly defining the natural and supernatural orders and their inter-relationships. We are recognizing the state of the soul without redemption, the original sinfulness of Adam, the consequent redemption in Christ, the God-man. Here is the answer to the easy perfectibility of man sponsored by Rousseau, to the self-reliance of man espoused by the naturalists, to the utter corruption of man and consequent pessimistic view found in Luther and the neo-orthodox theologians of our day.

The third doctrine, of Mary's Assumption, defined in 1950 by Pius XII, answers a long accumulation of errors regarding man's body and its relative place in the focus of eternity. Materialism seems a poor substitute for the fullness of truth when we see Mary receiving in advance the wonderful victory over concupiscence and death that is promised to all of us on the last day at the Resurrection of the body. The body is not merely animal—of the earth, earthly—but is to be united to the victory of the soul in eternal bliss where human emotions are spiritualized and exalted forever.

In all of these doctrines we see Mary as the prototype of what we Christians are meant to be: Christ-bearers freed from the influence of sin and evil, eternal sharers in the fullness of our humanity, body and soul, with the victory of Christ and Mary at the end of time. She brings us the reality of this promise in herself and in what we believe her to be as a human being: Mother of God, conceived immaculate, assumed bodily into heaven. Surely she alone, in the Providence of God, has, by being what she is, "destroyed all heresy."

There are two final chapters to this book. Both are historical in nature, for we believe that, after seeing the doctrinal justification of Mary's place in Catholic life, our fellow Americans would better appreciate her place in the history of our country and in the life of the University that bears her name and presents this volume.

These papers were first read as lectures addressed to the faculty and student body of the University of Notre Dame, during the autumn of 1954. They are presented here in the form in which they were delivered.

May these pages speak honorably of Mary, and bring others to the realization that in the Providence of God this humble maid of Nazareth speaks yet today with a voice that can lead all of us to ultimate victory over all that threatens humanity in time and in eternity.

THEODORE M. HESBURGH, C.S.C.
President
University of Notre Dame

The Mystery
of the Woman

REJOICE, O VIRGIN MARY,
WHO HAST TRIUMPHED SINGLE-HANDED
OVER EVERY HERESY IN THE WHOLE WORLD

Theotokos:

The Mother of God

WALTER J. BURGHARDT, S.J.
WOODSTOCK COLLEGE
WOODSTOCK, MARYLAND

Theotokos: The Mother of God

One of the most significant sermons of antiquity was delivered fifteen centuries ago. The date: early September, 431. The place: the Church of St. Mary at Ephesus on the west coast of Asia Minor. The congregation: almost 200 bishops of the East. The occasion: the dying hours of the Council of Ephesus, at which a virgin of Nazareth was proclaimed Mother of God. The preacher: Cyril, Patriarch of Alexandria in Egypt.

Cyril opened his sermon with a startling eulogy: "Hail, from us, Mary, Mother of God, majestic treasure of the whole world . . . crown of virginity, sceptre of orthodoxy . . . dwelling of the Illimitable, mother and virgin. . . ." Cyril closed his sermon with a remarkable sentence: "May we . . . reverence the undivided Trinity, while we sing the praise of the ever-virgin Mary, that is to say, the holy Church, and of her spotless Son and Bridegroom." [1]

The two facets of this lecture are suggested by two appositive phrases with which Cyril dignifies Mary: (*a*) "Mary, Mother of God," and (*b*) "Mary, that is to say, the holy Church." More specifically, I submit that the significance of the divine maternity in 431, when it was equivalently defined, lay in its relationship to the *physical* Christ; and that its significance in 1954 lies in its relationship to the *mystical* Christ. In other words, the significance of the divine maternity in fifth-century Ephesus lay primarily in this, that it furnished a fresh insight into the *person* of Christ, into Christology; its added significance in twentieth-century America lies in this, that it suggests a fresh insight into the *work* of Christ, into soteriology.

First, then, 431. The Council of Ephesus is significant for a fact, and the fact itself has significance. The *fact* is simple enough. The title, Mother of God (*theotókos*), was expressly presented to the Council, in a letter of Cyril, as orthodox doctrine, and Cyril's letter was solemnly approved in the assembly.[2] This impressive approbation did not fall like a thunderclap on the Christian world; it had been prepared by three and a half centuries of theological development. That development is itself fascinating.[3]

Strangely enough, what was first denied to Our Lady after she left this earth was not the prerogative, Mother of *God,* but what her contemporaries never dreamed of denying, that she was Mother of *Jesus.* The early crisis was Docetic—the affirmation that our Savior simply did not have a genuinely human body, or at any rate, as Tertullian sums it up, that "He was born *through* a virgin, not *of* a virgin—*in* a womb, not *of* a womb." [4] In a word, He was not fashioned of Mary's substance. But there was a complementary denial. Where the Gnostics introduced a distinction between Jesus born of Mary and the Christ who

6

descended into Jesus at baptism, they denied implicitly that the Child of Mary was God.

The Christian reaction in the first three centuries is expressive. Not that our Lady is categorically denominated Mother of God; there is no indisputable evidence for the title before the fourth century. But Ignatius and Aristides in the East, Justin and Irenaeus and Tertullian in the West, have a two-edged answer for the Gnostic position. On the one hand, they use expressions that equivalently affirm Mary's divine motherhood. On the other, they trumpet the twin premises for their conclusion: (*a*) Jesus was genuinely born of Mary; and (*b*) Jesus born of Mary is God.

With the fourth century the title, *Mother of God,* becomes a commonplace. As the evidence stands, we find it first in 319, when Alexander, Bishop of Alexandria, announces to his colleagues the deposition of Arius.[5] But even then the word flows from his pen so naturally, so spontaneously—I might almost say, so nonchalantly—that it leaves an impression of everyday usage. And soon the Christian world echoes with it. Athanasius in Alexandria, Eusebius in Caesarea, Cyril in Jerusalem, Epiphanius in Salamis, Hilary in Gaul, Ambrose in Milan, and Jerome in Rome—none feels he must justify it, none feels there is something to explain. So welcome is the word that in 382 Gregory of Nazianzus can hurl anathema at Apollinaris: "If anyone does not admit that holy Mary is Mother of God, he is separated from the divinity." [6] And while the theologian wielded the word as a weapon, the layman whispered it in accents of love. For from the same fourth century comes a precious papyrus leaf, from which we can

Theotokos: The Mother of God 7

reconstruct the original Greek of our lovely prayer, "We fly to thy patronage, O holy Mother of God"; and the word that stands out clearly is *theotóke,* Mother of God.[7] More eloquent than this love-call of Christians is Julian the Apostate's cry of despair: "You [Christians] never stop calling Mary Mother of God."[8]

Little wonder that, from 428 on, a rising reluctance to call Mary, "Mother of God" provoked such violent reactions. Little wonder that, when Nestorius of Constantinople gave his blessing to a bishop who preached, "If anyone says that holy Mary is Mother of God, let him be anathema," Cyril of Alexandria retorted, "If anyone does *not* confess that . . . the holy Virgin is Mother of God . . . let him be anathema."[9] Little wonder that, when the Council of Ephesus convened in 431, Cyril could write of that first session to his flock in Alexandria:

"Know, then, that on the [22nd of June] the holy Synod met at Ephesus in the great Church . . . of Mary, Mother of God. We spent the whole day there, and finally . . . we deposed . . . Nestorius and removed him from the episcopal office. Now there were about 200 (more or less) of us bishops gathered together. And the whole populace of [Ephesus] was waiting tensely, waiting from dawn to dusk for the decision of the holy Synod. When they heard that the unfortunate fellow had been deposed, with one voice all started to shout in praise of the holy Synod, with one voice all began to glorify God, because the enemy of the faith had fallen. When we left the church, they escorted us to our lodging with torches; for it was evening. Gladness was in the air; lamps dotted the city; even women went before us with censers and led the way."[10]

That is the *fact* of Ephesus, and on the surface it is

simple enough. A bishop had questioned Mary's most precious prerogative, and his brother bishops had banned him from their fellowship. But that is not quite the *significance* of Ephesus. Nestorius' concept of Mary stemmed from his concept of Christ. Similarly, what Ephesus determined with respect to Mary's motherhood was rooted in what Ephesus believed with respect to Christ's sonship. That is why Nestorius, for all his reluctance, could say to Cyril in all honesty: "It is not on the ground of a [mere] name that I part from you; it is on the essence of God the Word and on the essence of the Man." [11] What was at stake was the Incarnation itself. In what sense did God become man? In what sense can we say with St. John, "the Word was made flesh"? How were God and human nature made one in the womb of a virgin?

The solution of Nestorius is shrouded in uncertainty. How he conceived that incredible union is not at all clear; somehow God dwelt in flesh as in a temple. What is clear is the set of conclusions he drew therefrom. "Does God have a mother? [He does not.]" "I say it is the flesh that was born of the Virgin Mary, not God the Word. . . ." "It is not right to say of God that He sucked milk. . . ." "I do not say that God is two or three months old." "A born God, a dead God, a buried God I cannot adore." [12]

The answer of Ephesus was unequivocal. The flesh which Mary fashioned of her flesh, that flesh the Son of God took to Himself, took as His own, at the moment of its fashioning. At that instant, and forevermore, this flesh was as much God's flesh as my flesh is mine. This union of God's Son with a human nature was a far different thing from the presence of God in every corner of His universe, far different from His presence in my soul through grace, far different from His presence in my body through Communion, far different even from the Nestorian idea of God dwelling in a temple. This flesh fashioned of Mary is the only flesh that is strictly God's own. When Mary murmured, "Be it done unto me according to thy word," at that moment there were not two individuals, two persons in her womb: one of them God, the other a man. There was one individual, one person: the God-Man. The Man was God, and God was the Man.

That is why Ephesus could believe, against Nestorius, that *God* was conceived in Mary's womb and lay for nine months beneath her heart; that *God* was laid in a feeding-trough and exiled to Egypt; that *God* worked with His hands, learned what hunger tastes like, and thirst; that *God* was tired enough to sleep out a storm in an open boat; that *God* was slapped and spat upon, mocked for a fool, whipped like a dog, and nailed to a tree.

The Man was God, and God was the Man. That is why Ephesus had to believe that the thoughts of Christ which cover the pages of the Gospel, the words which fell for thirty years from the lips of Christ, are God's thoughts and God's words. Not that God somehow reached out and claimed them, called them His own; but that these thoughts were framed in the human mind of God, these words hung on the human lips of God. It was not a man linked to God like other men, who whipped traffickers from a temple, who loved Martha and her sister Mary, who wept over Jerusalem and over Lazarus. It was God enfleshed.

It is only if you hold fast to this concept of Christ that you can call Mary unconditionally Mother of God; Nestorius saw that. And conversely, it is only if you cling unequivocally to the title, Mother of God, that you can find the Son of God in a human womb; Nestorius saw that too.

That is why Ephesus canonized the letter to Nestorius in which Cyril declared: "We must not . . . sever into two sons the one Lord Jesus Christ. Such severance will be no help at all to the correct expression of the faith, even if one allege unity of persons. Scripture, you see, has not said that the Word united to Himself the person of a man, but that He has been made flesh. Now the Word's being made flesh is nothing else than that He partook of flesh and blood in like manner with us, and made our body His own, and proceeded Man of a woman, without having cast away His divinity. . . . This is what the expression of the exact faith everywhere preaches; this is the mind we shall find in the holy Fathers. In this sense they did not hesitate to call the holy Virgin God's Mother (*theotókos*)—not as though the nature of the Word or His divinity took beginning of being from the holy Virgin, but that of her was begotten the holy body animated with a rational soul; to this body the Word was united personally, and so He is said to have been born according to the flesh." [13]

Briefly, then, Mary is Mother of God. She is Mother, because the flesh God took, He took from her flesh; and because Mary gave to her Son everything any mother gives to her child in its fashioning. She was pregnant with Christ. And she is Mother of God, simply because the human being who came forth from her womb was and is God.

It is understandable, then, why Ephesus was so exercised over a single word, *theotókos*. True, in the minds of some reputable historians Ephesus is synonymous with imprudence, intrigue, ecclesiastical politics. But, to its credit, Ephesus recognized that the denial or even the abandonment of *theotókos* was equivalent to a disavowal of Nicaea.

Not that the Council of Nicaea had called Mary "Mother of God"; but that, unless Mary is God's Mother, you cannot confess, with the Fathers of Nicaea, "I believe in . . . Jesus Christ, God's Son . . . who for us men and for our salvation came down, was made flesh, became man. . . ." [14]

Call Ephesus, if you will, a war of words; we need not blush. For us, a word is the incarnation of an idea. A century before, in the Arian crisis, the Christian world had been ruptured by a word. With that word, *homooúsios,* "consubstantial," Athanasius summed up orthodox belief on the Eternal Word, the Son of God. In the Nestorian controversy the Christian East was sundered once more by a word. With that word, *theotókos,* "Mother of God," Cyril summed up orthodox belief on the Word Incarnate, the Son of God made flesh. That is why Cyril could thunder: "To confess our faith in orthodox fashion . . . it is enough to . . . confess that the holy Virgin is Mother of God." [15] And three centuries later St. John Damascene, whose glory it is to have summed up in himself the theology of the Greek Fathers, wrote so simply: "This name contains the whole mystery of the Incarnation." [16]

It is a striking thing that a Mariological term should have been selected as the ultimate test of Christological orthodoxy. Striking, but not surprising. Our Lady's role at Ephesus is the spontaneous outgrowth of her role at Nazareth, of her role throughout history. Her deep significance has always been her relationship to Christ. At Ephesus it was the *physical* Christ her divine maternity revealed. In this human mother the Christian mind caught a vision of her divine Son.

12

So much for 431. It is the contention of this lecture that in 1954 the divine maternity has an added significance. In 431 the significance of Mary's motherhood lay in its relationship to the *physical* Christ; in 1954 its significance lies in its relationship to the *mystical* Christ. At Ephesus the divine maternity furnished a fresh insight into the *person* of Christ, into Christology, into the fact of the Incarnation; in 1954 it suggests a fresh insight into the *work* of Christ, into soteriology, into the task of the redemption.

You see, in theological circles today there is a remarkable Marian movement. What this movement yearns for is a deeper penetration into the mystery that is Mary, the mystery that makes Mary the unique creature she is. It is not content to see in the Mother of God simply the object of a special veneration, of a warmer flame of love. It wants to insert our Lady in her proper place in the divine dream for our redemption.

To achieve this, theologians are aware that it is not sufficient to range privilege alongside privilege, mystery beside mystery, and say: that is Mary. It is not enough to plumb the depths of Mary's Immaculate Conception, her perpetual virginity, her divine maternity, her utter sinlessness, her glorious Assumption; it is not enough to penetrate the meaning and the beauty of each of these if you are to say: I know Our Lady. For beauty and truth lie not so much in the isolated fragments as in the harmony of the whole. What is needed is a basic idea which gives meaning to all the rest, some tremendous insight into the mind of God which, while it welds together the scattered prerogatives that spell Mary, will, above all, explain her role in the divine design we designate redemption.

Basically, I believe, this insight will have to be achieved in terms of the divine maternity; that prerogative is, in some genuine sense, fundamental. But the contemporary theologian is asking: Is there something still more fundamental? What is it that lies at the core of Mary's motherhood? Why, for example, did God fashion Mary precisely as bridal Mother of God—as God's Mother and His bride as well? God wills it, yes; but God's will is not whim. It may be that we shall end by bending low before mystery. The point, however, is this: theologians believe they have caught a glimpse of the divine idea that gives ultimate meaning to the divine maternity, that sets the Mother of God in the center of God's plan for man.

The solution to the problem was suggested towards the close of the fourth century by St. Ambrose, Bishop of Milan, when he wrote: "Mary is type of the Church." [17] To have a type—as we are using the word here—four elements are desirable. In the first place, you have concrete representation, even at times personification. An idea, a spiritual reality is represented by something concrete, is represented by some palpable form, is made present at times by a human figure. Somewhat as we represent, personify the abstract idea of justice by a blindfolded lady with scales and a sword, so the early Christians represented, personified the inner life of the Church by the human figure of our Lady.

The second requisite: a real relationship that links the two, an objective foundation for this representation. The relationship that links Mary and the Church, the relationship that makes Mary a type of the Church, is not a creation of the human mind, as is the case with justice and the visionless lady in white. It is not a casual, accidental

14

likeness which invites the meditative mind to oscillate between Mary and the Church. The resemblance between the
Church and the human figure of Mary is the consequence
of an inner tie that is real, a deep-seated relation that is objective. The resemblance between the two is not put there
by the human mind; it *is* there. The relationship is not in-
vented; it is discovered.

The third requisite is the most significant, if only because it concretizes the second. A type cannot rest satis-
fied with two terms, the type and the antitype, the figure
and the thing it prefigures, the human person and the spiritual reality it personifies. It demands a third term, a design
which envelops the other two, a master-plan which finds its
first realization and revelation in the person who is the type,
and its second revelation and realization in the antitype. In
the concrete, when we say that Mary is type of the Church,
we do not isolate Mary and the Church, as though they
were related in some sort of vacuum. Mary is type of the
Church in virtue of a divine design, an eternal plan in the
mind of God which finds its realization first in bodily form
in the person of Mary, then in the spiritual reality that is
the Church. The resemblance between Mary and the
Church is rooted in the divine dream of redemption. The
third term is God—God's plan for man.

The fourth element follows from the second and third:
the prototype is a moral pattern for the image. A *moral*
pattern. The prototype, Mary, is a living individual. The
image, the Church, is a collectivity, is actualized in the individuals who make up the Mystical Body of Christ. If
Mary, as type of the Church, personifies the inmost essence
of the Church, if the Church that unfolds in space and time
exists in germ in Mary, then Mary is the model for the con-

duct of the Christian, the pattern of Christian living. Briefly, if by divine design Mary realizes in her own person what the Church is destined by God to be, then by divine design Mary realizes in her own life what the Christian is destined by God to do.

That much premised, the present lecture will put forward a fact and an explanation. The fact: Mary is, in God's redemptive design, a prototype of the Church. The explanation: what this means in the concrete, how the Mary-Church idea lends meaning to the Mother of God and to her role in redemption.

First, then, is Mary a prototype of the Church? Did God plan redemption in such a way that, before the Church came forth from the pierced side of God's Son on Calvary, this Church somehow found its first realization in God's Mother? The answer will issue not from speculation but from revelation. God's mind is manifest in God's word.

In the twelfth chapter of the Apocalypse St. John has his celebrated Vision of the Woman. "In heaven a great portent appeared: a woman that wore the sun for her mantle, with the moon under her feet, and a crown of twelve stars about her head. She had a child in her womb, and was crying out as she travailed, in great pain of her delivery. Then a second portent appeared . . . : a great dragon . . . fronting the woman . . . ready to swallow up the child as soon as she bore it. She bore a son, the son who is to herd the nations with a crook of iron. . . . In his spite against the woman, the dragon went elsewhere to make war on the rest of her children, the men who keep God's commandments, and hold fast to the truth concerning Jesus." [18]

Many Scripture scholars insist that in the woman of Apocalypse 12 you have the Church of God personified.[19]

16

This woman, who has a vast progeny, whose children are the human beings who believe in Christ and live that belief, must be the Church of God. But this woman, who personifies the Church, is apparently the Mother of Christ: her son, says John, "is to herd the nations like sheep with a crook of iron." The Church of Christ, then, is personified by a woman, and the woman is the Mother of Christ. Somehow, therefore, in God's eyes, the Church and Mary are one.

This basic idea, that Mary is a type of the Church, recurs in patristic literature, in the theology of the first seven centuries, with an impressive constancy.[20] In the first place, the Fathers frequently describe the Church in language borrowed from the person of Mary. The Church, like Mary, is a virgin. The Church, Origen insists, "is a chaste virgin, by reason of her rectitude in belief and in morality." [21] The Church, like Mary, is a virgin mother. "Mary," says Augustine, "gave birth in body to the Head of this body; the Church gives birth in spirit to the members of that Head. In both [Mary and the Church], virginity is no hindrance to fertility; in both, fertility does not displace virginity." [22] The Church's virginal motherhood, like Mary's, involves a sponsal relationship: the Church, like Mary, is bride of God. Christ our Lord, Jerome remarks, "is bridegroom of the virgin Church—the Church which has neither spot nor wrinkle." [23] And though the Church's childbearing is consummated externally in baptism, as Mary's was in Bethlehem, at the basis of both is an inner act of conception: Christ is conceived in the soul of the Christian, as He was conceived in the body of Mary, in that the soul, like Mary, hears the word of God and believes it. In both there is a pregnant fiat: "Be it done unto me according to thy word."

"That," as Chrysostom has it, "that is how the Church is wed to God." [24]

But the Fathers go further. They are not content to dignify the Church with the prerogatives of Mary; such a manner of speaking might be sheer metaphor. The Fathers are more explicit than that; they tell us it is more than metaphor. Some insist that God deliberately made the Church like His Mother. As Augustine puts it: "The most beautiful among the sons of men [is] the Son of holy Mary, the Bridegroom of holy Church. Her [the Church] He made like to His Mother, for He made her our mother and keeps her His virgin." [25] "Our Head," he claims, "had to be born of a virgin . . . in the way of the flesh, as a sign that His members were to be born of a virgin Church in the way of the spirit." [26] Some Fathers are more explicit still; they declare expressly that our Lady is type of the Church. Listen to Ambrose: "It is well that [Mary] is betrothed and yet a virgin, for she is type of the Church, which though wed is spotless." [27] And Ephraem, the most distinguished representative of Syrian Christianity: "The Virgin Mary is a prototype of the Church, because she received the beginnings of the Gospel." [28] And with no hesitation, no equivocation, comes the uncompromising affirmation: Mary and the Church are one; somehow Mary is the Church. Ephraem, for example, emphasizes the fact that beneath the cross Christ "gave to John Mary, His Church." [29] Cyril of Alexandria we have heard at Ephesus: "May we reverence the undivided Trinity, while we sing the praise of the ever-virgin Mary, that is to say, the holy Church." [30]

What Scripture hints at darkly, what the Fathers declare implicitly and explicitly, the Latin Middle Ages develop almost without interruption. Mary is type of the Church; she

18

is its figure; she signifies it. The mystery of the Church is contained in the mystery of Mary as in its prototype and perfect exemplar. It is at once still hidden there and already revealed in advance, because it finds there its first and ideal realization. Our Lady, therefore, announces the Church and precedes it. She is its anticipation, and the remarkable things God accomplished in her He does not cease to reproduce in the Church. From the one to the other there is a real continuity; we cannot separate them; Mary and the Church are inseparably linked, because the same Christ links them to Himself.[31]

The fact, therefore, seems beyond dispute. In Christian tradition Mary is type of the Church. So was she destined by God; so was she in actuality. The more difficult question remains: what does this mean in the concrete? How does the Mary-Church analogy lend meaning to the Mother of God and to her role in the drama of redemption?

The fundamental principle which dominates this whole discussion was formulated by St. Augustine: "He who made you without your cooperation does not justify you without your cooperation." [32] It is the principle of human cooperation in the divine task of redemption: God has determined to save man by means of man. As in Paradise, so on earth, as in man's original fall, so in his later restoration, God would respect the inmost nature of His human creation, man's perilous power to say no. That divine decision spangles the pages of the Old Testament. Salvation is presented as a covenant, a pact, a contract offered by God and accepted by man. Or it is a marriage, wide-eyed and free, nuptials of love between God and Israel, and, in the New Testament, between Christ and the Church. The basic datum of this symbolism, exploited in Christian tradition till the Renaissance, is significant. In this marriage God is everywhere and always the man, the bridegroom; humanity is everywhere and always the woman, the bride. In this inspired figure of salvation it is the male who symbolizes the initiative and the power of God; it is the female who symbolizes the active receptivity of humanity and the fruitfulness which union with God communicates to it.

God saves man by means of man. In line with that design, God *became* man, asked of humanity the free gift of its flesh and blood. In harmony with that plan, Christ leaves His Church, the prolongation of His Incarnation, in the hands of men. The book that bears His name—the word of God—comes line by line from the pen of men. The grace He has won with His own body is communicated through the hands and lips of men. Nor will He come to the human heart unless the human heart whispers, "Come."

Now this cooperation of man with God is exercised in two ways: by faith and by ministry. Faith is primarily an interior thing, a drama within the soul; ministry is an exterior thing, a communication, an administration of words and sacramental signs whereby faith is born and grows. Faith is the task of the whole Christian community; ministry is the privilege of a segment within that community. Faith is receiving, an active receptivity; ministry is giving, an exercise of power in the name of God.

Precisely here we reach a conclusion of supreme significance. Mary cannot be a type of the ministering Church, of the Church in its hierarchical function. The hierarchical aspect of the Church is rather a prolongation of Christ's own activity, Christ's own power. It is the divine in the Church. Our Lady is type of the human element in redemption; she represents the believing Church, the whole community of Christians, men and women, hierarchy and laity, in so far as it hears the word of God and welcomes it within.

This personification of the Church finds its crucial hour at the Annunciation. That first Angelus, so simply told by St. Luke, veils a tremendous truth. It was not simply that God wanted Mary's motherhood to be a voluntary thing, uncompelled, unconstrained. Gabriel's role is more profound than that. The Son of God was about to wed human nature to Himself. Therefore, as St. Thomas phrases it, "what God was asking through the Annunciation was the consent of the Virgin *in the name of all humanity*." [33] Or, in the lovely sentence of Leo XIII: "The eternal Son of God, when He wanted to take to Himself man's nature, and so enter a mystical marriage with the whole human race, did not do so before obtaining the perfectly free consent of His Mother-to-be, *who played as it were the role of the human race itself*." [34] And, while a world waited breathlessly, Mary answered, "Be it done unto me according to thy word." Mary said yes. That whispered yes may well have been, in God's eyes, Mary's finest hour. At that moment she became bride of God and His Mother too: bride of God by her fiat, Mother of God whom she welcomed in her womb. At that instant was realized in Mary the substance of the mystery of the Church to come: the union of God and man in the Mystical Body of Christ.

This welcome given God by Mary was not a sheerly passive thing; it was incredibly active on all levels. In the spiritual order her faith, like all genuine faith, was the quickening response of her mind to a manifestation of God. In the moral order her consent was the loving response of her will to an invitation of God. In the physical order her conception was the living response of her body to the activity of God: "the holy Spirit shall come upon thee."

Briefly, our Lady, as Mother of God and His bride, has a representative function. The task of the believing Church is to continue through space and time the sponsal fiat of Mary, her whispered yes. This community of the redeemed has for vocation to cooperate in the work of redemption by loving faith, and so bring God to birth in the human frame. The Church, therefore, is a collective Mary, and Mary is the Church in germ.

This vision of Mary's motherhood as a representative thing becomes clearer still if we see it in its virginal aspect. In our synthesis it is no longer satisfying to see in our Lady's virginity before and after Bethlehem little more than a privilege highly appropriate, perhaps indispensable in a girl who is God's Mother. It will not do to ask with St. Ambrose: "Would the Lord Jesus choose for Himself a mother who could defile heaven's court with the seed of man?" [35] From the vantage-ground of history the answer is no. But the question is perilous. It might well leave the impression that the marital relationship is something less than good. Or it might, in reaction, revive a seductive fourth-century error, to the effect that marriage and virginity are equal in honor, that (as Helvidius claimed) Mary is doubly admirable for having been, in turn, virgin and mother: virgin till the birth of Jesus, then mother of the "brothers and sisters of Jesus" spoken of in Scripture. In any event, though the rhetoric of Ambrose may stimulate piety, it does not satisfy theology. The divine design goes deeper than that. Even in her virginity Mary is type of the Church; she represents the community of believers; her virginal motherhood is a first, a concrete, a symbolic realization of God's plan for redeemed humanity.

Womanly virginity, you see, has two facets. Negatively, it denies that intimate relationship with man which we term marital; it denies the initiative of man with respect to woman and woman's fruitfulness. But virginity, in the Christian concept, is not sheer negation, the absence of something. The negative aspect of virginity stems from something positive. The denial to man of any initiative in her fruitfulness must, if it is to be Christian, stem from a woman's total dedication to God, a complete openness to the divine, receptivity to God and to God alone. The denial of a bridal relationship to man is rooted in the affirmation of a bridal relationship to God.

And so it was with Mary. Her virginity meant, on the one hand, that no human being, no man, took the initiative in the bridal relationship which issued in the Son of God made flesh: "the Holy Spirit shall come upon thee." It meant, on the other hand—in fact, the denial of human initiative stemmed from—the total consecration of Mary to her Bridegroom, utter cooperation with God, an unfailing fiat, complete and exclusive.

And in this Mary is type of the Church; she represents the community of believers; she realizes in her own person what God intended for redeemed humanity. On the one hand, this union of God with man which is the Church denies to man the initiative in the task which links man to God. Not that man is purely passive; he must cooperate, else oneness with God is impossible. But his cooperation is a response—a response to grace, a response to God's invitation. "If we but turn to God," Augustine insists, "that itself is a gift of God." [36] And that is the other aspect, the positive side, of the Church's virginity. The Church is linked to Christ as bride to groom. Her role, like that of Mary, is total consecration to Christ, a complete openness to the divine, a sensitiveness to the action of God's Spirit, an incredible readiness to respond, "Be it done unto me according to thy word."

The paradox is this. It is not simply that, as Augustine said, Mary's "virginity is no hindrance to fertility." For the Church as for Mary, it is only by reason of her virginity that she can achieve fertility. It was only by Mary's total response to God's invitation alone that the Son of God became flesh; it is only by prolonging this response through space and time that the Church, impregnated with the Spirit, is fruitful for the formation of Christ in individual souls. The words of Gabriel are expressive: "The Holy Spirit shall come upon thee and the power of the Most High shall overshadow thee; and *therefore* the Holy One to be born shall be called the Son of God."

This vision of Mary's virginal motherhood as a representative thing grows clearer still if we ponder her Immaculate Conception. Here, too, our Lady is type of the Church. The Church, remember, is the Body of Christ. But it is a body redeemed; the members of that body have been touched with redemption. In the concrete, a human being enters the Church at a specific moment in time, by a baptism which weds him to Christ as it incorporates him into the Body of Christ. At that instant he *is* a person redeemed—at the instant he enters the Church. His redemption, however, has twin facets. Positively, he has captured Christ's life; negatively, he no longer has original sin. The two cannot coexist in the human soul: Christ's life and original sin. But notice: As God planned it, the Church

24

does not take the human being, incorporate him into the Body of Christ, into the Church, and *then* remove original sin. At the moment he enters the Church he *is* free of original sin. That is why we say: the Church is a community of the redeemed, not a community of those who are to be redeemed.

But if it is of the Church's essence to be a community of the redeemed, of those who are free from original sin, then the Church herself has no part in original sin. That is her God-given nature. Therefore, at the first moment of her existence, at the instant of her incarnation on Calvary, she was sinless. In the womb of humanity, in the midst of a world estranged from God by the sin of Adam, the Church was conceived without original sin.

Here, too, in God's staggering design, the Mother of God is type of the Church. For, if the Church is to be personified, the human figure who personifies it must, like the Church, be free of Adam's sin. And not simply freed after being burdened with it. If it is of the Church's essence to be without original sin, to have no part in it, then the individual who is type of the Church must be without sin from the first moment of her existence; she must be immaculately conceived. That person, alone among the children fashioned of human seed, is God's Mother. Mary conceived without sin is Mary redeemed; and Mary conceived without sin, Mary redeemed, prefigures the whole community of the redeemed which is the Church, fashioned without sin from the lanced side of the Crucified.

This vision of God's Mother as type of the Church grows in clarity if we study her perfect sinlessness, her freedom from actual sin. The inner essence of the Church, as community of the redeemed, means the participation of men in the redemption effected by Christ. All men who have been touched with redemption in baptism and are linked to the Church in submissive faith belong to this community of the redeemed. But redemption is a gradual process, a lifelong thing; it is not complete in baptism. We belong to this community of the redeemed more or less perfectly, we are more or less perfect members of the Church, to the extent that redemption has taken hold of us, in proportion as grace or sin dominates in our soul.

Because the redemption of humanity—in fact, the redemption of the individual—is not yet complete, the Church is not without sinners. Pius XII put it well: "One must not imagine that the Body of the Church, just because it bears the name of Christ, is made up during the days of its earthly pilgrimage only of members conspicuous for their holiness. . . . It is the Savior's infinite mercy that allows place in His Mystical Body here for those whom He did not exclude from the banquet of old." [37]

The Church is not without sinners, but it is without sin. "I believe in the holy Catholic Church." This is the Church which Paul saw Christ summoning into His own presence, "the Church in all its beauty, no stain, no wrinkle, no such disfigurement . . . holy . . . spotless." [38] A paradox, yes: a Church of the sinful, yet herself without sin.[39] But nonetheless true. Where the Church is, there sin is, because man, though redeemed from sin, is still free to sin. Sin, however, stands in contradiction to the Church's essence, and the Church's essence stands in contradiction to sin. But her essence, as community of the redeemed, will be fully realized only when redemption is complete, and sin is no more, and the Church looks upon her Head in

26

glory—the day when, as Augustine said, "there will be but one Christ loving Himself."

Here again God's Mother is type of the Church. In her soul redemption found its perfect realization; in her soul there was never sin, there was only God. In our Lady we see God's design for redeemed humanity; in her we discover in its ideal state the sinlessness which is of the Church's essence, yet is realized not at once, but from day to day, through sin upon sin, till humanity be gathered up in Christ.

This vision of God's Mother as personification of redeemed humanity finds a final clarity in her bodily assumption. There is a popular misconception among Christians with respect to the human body. For some, the body is nothing but an instrument, a tool of the soul. For others, the body is a burden from which the soul cries for release. All this is an echo of the third-century theory of Origen that the soul has been imprisoned in matter because it sinned in an earlier existence. Such an attitude pays slender homage to God. It fails to recognize that the body is an essential part of man, that without the body man is a creature incomplete; that, whether in heaven or purgatory or hell, a separated soul, as Jean Mouroux phrased it, "still longs for its body with a purely natural impulse of love." [40]

In somewhat the same way the visible structure of the Church is an essential part of the Church. Not merely because it is an instrument through which God's life is communicated to men. It is that, of course; but it is more. The Church is visible of her very nature because everything which is to absorb redemption must somehow be absorbed into the Church. As the body played its part in the first sin, as the body fell with the soul from God, so does the body yearn for redemption. In the inspired language of Paul, we "groan in our hearts, waiting for that adoption which is the ransoming of our bodies from their slavery." [41]

This redemption of the body, like all redemption, is achieved through the Body of Christ, through the Church. What is redeemed is absorbed into the Church, helps constitute her essence. That is why the Church is not simply a spiritual thing; she is visible, tangible, sensible, material. And when the body of man is absorbed into the visible structure of the Church, it ceases to be what St. Paul termed "the body of death"; it comes spiritually alive, because it is quickened by the Spirit of God. And the more fully grace permeates the Church and each member, the more intimately does the body partake of redemption, and the less the "law in my members" wars against the "law of my mind." This, however, is but the beginning of redemption. Redemption will find its consummation, its perfection, in the glory of the life to come—not merely in the soul's vision of God, but in the transfiguration of the body, when the whole material world will share in the perfection of redemption, and there will be "a new heaven and a new earth."

If Mary is type of the Church, of redeemed humanity, then this redemption of the body must appear in its perfection in her. The redemption operated by the Church will be consummated only after the general resurrection, when the body will be transformed, and the whole man, soul and body, will confront his Creator in an eternity of knowledge and love. That perfection of humanity redeemed, that consummation of the Church, finds its first purely human realization in the Mother of God, in Mary assumed into heaven, soul and body.

This vision of God's Mother as type of the Church has much to recommend it. To begin with, it preserves a perfect balance between Mary's humanness and her uniqueness. On the one hand, it curbs the anguished accusation, Mariolatry. Our Lady is seen as fully human. She is not equated with divinity, because she is essentially representative of humanity. She is not on a par with God the Redeemer, because she personifies man the redeemed. In her we glimpse not so much God's design for a single human being, as His plan for all human beings. If there is glory here and divinization, it is all humanity that is glorified in her, all humanity that is divinized. Granted she is, in Augustine's word, "supereminent" member of the Church; [42] she remains, for all that, a member. And still she is not depreciated. If it is true that she symbolizes humanity redeemed, that she represents in her person what God intended for the whole Church, it is equally true that redeemed humanity, God's plan for His Church, is realized in its perfection in no individual save her.

Secondly, this vision of Mary as type of the Church clarifies and unifies her role in redemption. In this synthesis there is no Marian prerogative that is merely "fitting," no need to range privilege alongside privilege with a more or less tenuous tie. Mary is the unique creature she is, because redemption is the unique program it is. Redemption is a master-plan, divinely conceived, divinely executed. It finds its first, its ideal, its perfect realization in a single human being: Mary redeemed. It finds its ultimate realization in a community of human beings: humanity redeemed.

What the Mother of God is, that the Church is destined to be. And what the Church is, that is already discoverable in God's Mother. When Léon Bloy saw the lesson of the Immaculate Conception in this, that the redemption was successful at its very outset, because it produced a Mary, he spoke more truly than he knew. For Mary is not simply redeemed; she is redeemed humanity.

Thirdly, this vision of Mary makes for authentic devotion. In attachment to the immaculate Virgin-Mother of God in glory, we are not simply bent low before mystery —mystery that is meaningless as far as contemporary living is concerned. We are not lost in wonder at an Immaculate Conception which can never be ours; at a wedding of perpetual virginity and physical motherhood unique in history; at a glorious resurrection not preluded, like ours, by the corruption of the tomb. Our devotion to God's Mother is the fruit not so much of mystery as of insight. In the Mother of God we encounter in human form the plan of God for man. In this one woman we see what the community of believers is and is destined to be. In her virginal maternity we glimpse in its perfection the role in which God casts every human being. What He asks of you and me is active receptivity—that, when we hear the word of God, we welcome it within. For on this depends our holiness, our oneness with God—the openness, the freedom with which we can respond, "Be it done unto me according to thy word."

NOTES

[1] Cyril of Alexandria, *Homiliae diversae* 4 (ed. E. Schwartz, *Acta concilioum oecumenicorum* 1, 1, 2, 104; *PG* 77, 996).

[2] In a recent attempt to determine the precise theological value of Ephesus' first session (June 22, 431), I. Ortiz de Urbina concludes that the divine maternity was expressly and directly defined; cf. "Il dogma di Efeso," in *Mélanges Martin Jugie* (Paris, 1953) 233–40.

[3] Cf., for example, W. J. Burghardt, "Mary in Western Patristic Thought," in J. B. Carol (ed.), *Mariology* 1 (Milwaukee, 1955) 109–55, esp. 132–37.

[4] Tertullian, *De carne Christi* 20 (*CSEL* 70, 238).

[5] Cf. Alexander of Alexandria, *Epist. ad Alexandrum Constant.* 12 (*PG* 18, 568).

[6] Gregory of Nazianzus, *Epist.* 101 (*PG* 37, 177).

[7] Cf. G. Vannucci, "La più antica preghiera alla Madre di Dio," *Marianum* 3 (1941) 97–101; O. Stegmüller, "*Sub tuum praesidium*: Bemerkungen zur ältesten Überlieferung," *Zeitschrift für katholische Theologie* 74 (1952) 76–82. M. Gordillo, like Vannucci, believes it more probable that the papyrus belongs to the third century; cf. *Mariologia orientalis* (Rome, 1954), p. 7 and note 56.

[8] Quoted by Cyril of Alexandria, *Contra Iulianum* 8 (*PG* 76, 901).

[9] Cyril of Alexandria, *Epist.* 17, 12 (*ACO* 1, 1, 1, 40; *PG* 77, 120).

[10] Cyril of Alexandria, *Epist.* 24 (*ACO* 1, 1, 1, 117–18; *PG* 77, 137).

[11] Nestorius, *Liber Heraclidis* 2, 1; my translation is based on the French version by F. Nau *et al., Le Livre d'Héraclide de Damas* (Paris, 1910) 171.

[12] *Nestorii sermo* (*ACO* 1, 5, 1, 30); *Liber Heraclidis* 2, 1 (tr. Nau 176); *Nestorii tractatus* (*ACO* 1, 5, 1, 38); J. F. Bethune-Baker, *Nestorius and His Teaching* (Cambridge, 1908) 71. Cf. also Nilus a S. B., *De maternitate divina b. Mariae semper virginis Nestorii Constantinopolitani et Cyrilli Alexandrini sententia* (Rome, 1944) 1–19.

[13] Cyril of Alexandria, *Epist.* 4, 6 (*ACO* 1, 1, 1, 28; *PG* 77, 48).

[14] Cf. Cyril of Alexandria, *Epist.* 1, 5–6 (*ACO* 1, 1, 1, 12–13; *PG* 77, 16). For the text of the Symbol of Nicaea, cf. I. Ortiz de Urbina, *El Símbolo Niceno* (Madrid, 1947) 21.

[15] Cyril of Alexandria, *Homiliae diversae* 15 (*PG* 77, 1093).

[16] John Damascene, *De fide orthodoxa* 3, 12 (*PG* 94, 1029).

[17] Ambrose, *Expositio evangelii secundum Lucam* 2, 7 (*CSEL* 32/4, 45).

[18] Apoc 12:1–17, Knox translation.

[19] For example, Bernard J. Le Frois, in his recent extended treatment of the problem, *The Woman Clothed with the Sun* (*Ap. 12*): *Individual or Collective?* (Rome, 1954), concludes: "St. John under the figure of the Woman depicts Mary as the perfect realization of the Church" (262).

[20] The most comprehensive investigation of this theme in the Fathers is to be found in A. Müller, *Ecclesia-Maria: Die Einheit Marias und der Kirche* (2nd ed., Fribourg, Switzerland, 1955).

[21] Origen, *In Ioan. frag.* 45 (*GCS,* Orig. 4, 520).

[22] Augustine, *De sancta virginitate* 2 (*PL* 40, 397).

[23] Jerome, *In Ieremiam* 1, 44 (*CSEL* 59, 36).

[24] Chrysostom, *In Ioan. hom.* 29, 3 (*PG* 59, 170).

[25] Augustine, *Serm.* 195, 2 (*PL* 38, 1018).

[26] Augustine, *De sancta virginitate* 6 (*PL* 40, 399).

[27] Cf. footnote 17.

[28] I have taken this sentence of Ephraem from Müller (*op. cit.* 152), who, strangely enough, does not indicate where the pertinent passage is to be found among the works of Ephraem.

[29] Ephraem, *Ev. conc. exp.* (ed. Mösinger 134).

[30] Cf. footnote 1.

[31] For this summary of medieval thought on Mary and the Church I am indebted to H. Barré, "Marie et l'église dans la pensée médiévale," *Vie spirituelle* 91 (1954) 124–41.

[32] Augustine, *Serm.* 169, 13 (*PL* 38, 923).

[33] St. Thomas, *Summa theologica* 3, q. 30, a. 1 c.

[34] Leo XIII, Encyclical, *Octobri mense,* Sept. 22, 1891; *ASS* 24 (1891–92) 195.

[35] Ambrose, *De institutione virginis* 6, 4 (*PL* 16, 331).

[36] Augustine, *De gratia et libero arbitrio* 5, 10 (*PL* 44, 888).

[37] Pius XII, Encyclical, *Mystici corporis,* June 29, 1943; *AAS* 35 (1943) 203; official English translation, *The Encyclical* Mystici Corporis *of Pope Pius XII* (New York: America Press, 1943) 12.

[38] Eph 5:26–27; Knox translation.

[39] The problem is real and does not admit of any facile solution. For two engaging approaches, cf. C. Journet, *L'église du Verbe Incarné* 2 (Bruges, 1951) 1115–29; R. Hasseveldt, *The Church: A Divine Mystery,* translated by W. Storey (Chicago, 1954) 243–51.

[40] Jean Mouroux, *The Meaning of Man,* translated by A. H. G. Downes (New York, 1948) 108.

[41] Rom 8:23; Knox translation.

[42] Augustine, *Serm. Denis* 25, 7 (ed. Morin, *Miscellanea Agostiniana* [Rome, 1930] 1, 163).

The Immaculate Conception

FERRER SMITH, O.P.
DOMINICAN HOUSE OF STUDIES
WASHINGTON, D.C.

The Immaculate Conception

O n December 8th, 1854, in the Bull *Ineffabilis Deus*
Pope Pius IX thus expressed the teaching of the Church:

> We declare, announce, and define that the doctrine
> which states that the Blessed Virgin Mary was pre-
> served, in the first instant of her conception, by a
> singular grace and privilege of God Omnipotent and
> because of the merits of Jesus Christ the Savior of the
> human race, free from all stain of original sin, is re-
> vealed by God and must therefore be believed firmly
> and with constancy by all the faithful.[1]

Mary is immaculate by the merits of her Son. "Christ
died for all," says St. Paul, "in order that they who are
alive may live no longer for themselves, but for Him who
died for them and rose again." [2] In Mary and in her Immaculate Conception the redemption of Christ achieves its
greatest triumph. In other men the laver of Christ's mercy
liberates from sin contracted; in Mary it preserves her soul
free and pure of any stain. In the traditional examples of the
theologians, it is greater to ward off a blow than heal that

blow's effect; greater to prevent from falling into the mud than cleanse the fall's resultant mark. By her Immaculate Conception Mary is not removed from the ranks of the redeemed; in her, redemption is the most complete.

Original sin comes to us from Adam, for in him we have sinned and we are of his seed by generation. No sin was found in Christ nor possible to Him, for His human nature was formed by the action of the Holy Ghost and in a virgin; moreover in Him human nature was united to the very person of the Word of God. Mary, however, was the fruit of human union, her nature hers by human generation. Yet at the first instant when her soul was united to the body formed of tainted seed, God intervened. The debt was there and it was due to Mary that, like every child of Adam, her soul be infected by sin and without grace. The debt never became a fact. The infection was prevented by God Omnipotent and from the first instant of her being human, being Mary, her soul was filled with grace.

In Mary's Immaculate Conception all the great truths of revelation converge, find unity, reveal their wisdom. In Mary's Immaculate Conception the realities that bind men to God—creation, elevation, grace, redemption— attain their greatest realization in a pure creature. In the light of Mary's sanctity can the devastation caused by sin most accurately be gauged.

The Immaculate Conception and Sin

"We define that . . . in the first instant of her conception the Blessed Virgin Mary was preserved free from all stain of original sin." So to be free of sin is the first and most obvious meaning of the Immaculate Conception. So we who, to our sorrow, know of sin, first know Mary, not by what she is, but by what she is not. The beginning of Mary's life turns back our minds to the beginning of human life upon this earth. We take the first step in penetrating the purity of Mary's origin by knowing the stain that mars our own.

In man's creation God gave His gifts with divinely lavish hand. He gave the earth into man's care: "Let him have dominion over the fishes of the sea and the birds of the air, and the beasts and the whole earth." [3] Adam manifested that dominion in the naming of everything with full knowledge of its nature and its place in the created order. God gave him a body not subject to sickness, not subject to death. He enriched his human nature with passions perfectly controlled by reason; He enriched his mind with truth.

Yet not in these did God constitute man's happiness, man's fulfillment. These gifts of integrity were perfective of man's nature as such and were but the disposition to the more perfect reception, the more perfect living of the life of grace. To dwell in Paradise, to exercise dominion over the creatures of God, to be in possession of self, these but afforded man release, freedom to live with God, to live for God.

All the powers of the universe, all the capacities of man's nature were integrated, harmonized, unified toward one end: that man might will the will of God. God gave to Adam a will made perfect in being one with His. From that unity, from that identification, from that subjection all else flowed forth. It was at once the sign and measure of the resplendent transformation that made holy the very soul of Adam: his sanctifying grace. It was the channel allowing passage of the infinite goodness, the infinite love of God. Through it would pass riches without end and eternally. Through it God would pour out divinity, pour out Himself.

By his sin man damned up that channel, closed off the source of enrichment. By his sin he condemned himself to fight the earth for his livelihood, to fight his body for the freedom of his soul, to fight his passions for the possession of himself. By his sin he was divided from God, not one with Him; by his sin he was alone and lonely, not identified with God; by his sin he chose rebellion and the condition of hell, forfeited the subjection and hence the happiness of heaven.

The effects of that first sin have been exaggerated and minimized, been made the object more of mystification than of mystery. Yet they are not remote from us, for we are born with them, as inheritance of Adam. Moreover, the results of original sin are not essentially so different from the effects of our personal, actual sins as to lack all interpretation by means of personal experience. Mortal sin, original or personal, is first of all effective of what its very name expresses, death. Sin is the death, the ceasing to be of the supernatural life. The body without the soul is but a corpse, emptied of that which gave it being and identity, which made the distinction of its limbs and organs meaningful, which made of it a whole, a totality, possessed of harmony and beauty. Without the soul the body is destined to disintegration and decay, and however efficacious be the artificial means to stay that end, they cannot replace the soul, give life again, or prevent the earth from ultimately claiming its own dust.

Yet this is but the figure of the devastation of the soul by sin. The sanctifying grace that gave it supernatural being and identity with God is lost. Natural life remains and the powers proper to nature, but they are bereft of meaningfulness; they cannot of themselves produce the works of God. The powers, the capacities of man were distinguished one from another and multiplied that the life of man might be thereby enriched, that the love of God by grace might permeate man's whole being and give it wholeness, fullness, harmony and beauty. By the rebellion of sin man is despoiled of grace, and that rebellion spreads throughout the life of man. What were to be the instruments of enrichment become the focal points of conflict and source of the continual impoverishment of man's spirit.

Man remains man, with soul and body, possessed of the ability to know and love, feel joy and sorrow, experience desire. Sin cannot destroy these; indeed, sin cannot of itself exist unless man be man. For in sin is more denial than affirmation; it is a privation, a lack of what can and ought to be. As a crippled limb demands the leg it twists and fills with pain, so sin demands that man be man that it may distort his manhood and fill his life with misery.

Man remains man but turned aside from God. Not willing God he must yet will something and, if not God, a creature, ultimately himself. The goal man wills affects every aspect of his living. If he will God then he can find a place for all since all things are from God and to His glory. If he will creature he must eventually distort himself and everything. With his willing of God his power to know rejoices in truth and by truth expands and gives ever new dimension to his living. With his willing of sin the power to know must needs ignore the truth, gradually be blinded, suborned to error. With his willing of God his animal desires find a fulfillment more exalted than their own. With the willing of sin these same desires find themselves without restraint and hurry to enslave what should be master. Man remains man but without the supernatural life and with virtue replaced by the inclination to evil, to vice.

Original sin differs from actual sin in this, that it is a sin of nature. The grace given by God to man in man's creation was given to human nature in the person of Adam. By the first sin, of pride and disobedience, human nature was despoiled. The effects of sin became the condition of that nature. The supernatural life and the special gifts of nature for the living of that life, the gifts of integrity, were lost. "Through one man sin entered into the world and through sin death, and thus death has passed into all men because all have sinned." [4] Human nature remained human, of body and soul, of powers of spirit and flesh, yet supernaturally dead. The soul not resplendent with santifying grace but stained with sin, the will not subject to God but turned from Him, the mind not filled with truth nor eager for it but ignorant and prone to error, the passions of man bent on their own satisfaction—this was the human nature left to Adam after sin and come to us as we are his children, born of him. Truly we are the children of wrath, turned from divine benevolence, not only lacking grace but in sin; not only exiled from the Kingdom of God but under the sway of Satan.

To the destitution of sin Mary's Immaculate Conception offers sublime contrast. Never for an instant was she subject to Satan, subject of sin. Her soul was resplendent with a divine beauty, ordered entirely to God. Her every action took its vitality, its perfection from the principle

44

of that order, her sanctifying grace. She was free in freedom's richest, noblest meaning, to will and do only the best. No ignorance could blind, no error distort, her knowledge of God or of the creatures of God; her mind grew as truth was fed, enlarged and made yet deeper by wisdom. She judged all things in God and so her wisdom was divine, a part of His. The propulsive energy of passion could not distract, much less govern her; rather did her virtue make each act a total giving of herself to God. Of all women, of all purely human beings, she was and is the most alive. She is all in God and God is all in her and so does she confront forever the nothingness of death, of sin.

The Immaculate Conception and Divine Grace

Mary is all in God and God is all in her by grace. In this consists her splendor, her perfection. Grace is the reality in Mary, of Mary by which her soul was pleasing to God; indeed, of all created spirits the most pleasing. By the grace of the virtues her every capacity was turned to God, dedicated to and absorbed by His love and service. By the grace of the gifts of the Holy Ghost Mary was ready, even eager, to live by every illumination, every inspiration of the Spirit who was to be her Spouse. The Immaculate Conception is not defined in itself by a negation. Mary is without sin and so we know what she is not. She is filled with grace and by grace we know her as she is. The second step of penetrating the meaning of the Immaculate Conception must be found in the understanding of the grace of God.

Centuries ago the great bishop, St. John Chrysostom, spoke these words: "Should I be proud? Proud of face or form or figure or charm of body? With age they crumble, with death they decay. Should I be proud of knowledge, learning, erudition? As the years pass memory fails; as the years go on I grow more convinced of ignorance, of little learned, and vast riches of truth undreamed of. Should I be proud of works, feats, accomplishments? Only God will remember them. If they were done in pride, they are shameful monuments of sin; if they were done in God, then they are His and why should I be proud? Should I be proud of love? How can I when I am loved infinitely and in return but fail?"

"I am loved infinitely." Upon that realization is founded a true humility. "I am loved infinitely." Upon that truth is founded every confidence and every strength. Upon that truth rests the hope that carries man from earth to heaven, that draws its power from Omnipotence, its goodness from the goodness of God. "I am loved infinitely." Therein is the key to the meaning of grace.

What is grace? It is the love of God. The love of man supposes the good it loves. It finds the delicate beauty of a flower and cherishes the goodness so discovered. It sees the gracefulness of the bird and hears the sweetness of its song and loves the good thus revealed to it. The love of man finds honor, loyalty, sympathy in fellow man and opens its heart to embrace that goodness. The love of God supposes nothing, discovers nothing. The love of God creates, brings forth, the good. The love of God is the will of God willing the good to be, giving it reality, existence. In love God spoke the word *Fiat* and the world was and continues to be. All creation is, and literally, a divine love song; it is and moves and has its being by the loving will of God.

Beyond the love of God for stone and bird and flower

46

is the love of God for man. Of all material creation man is the chosen object of God's special love. That love too is creative, for divine love cannot be otherwise. The love of God for man creates in man a participation of divinity, a partaking of the life of God, a supernatural being, a supernatural life. And this is grace.

To gain the grace of God is to pass from death to life, from non-being to being. Once Jesus entered into the house of Jairus. [5] A tumult was being made and there was weeping and wailing, for the daughter of Jairus was dead. But Jesus put forth the multitude and taking with Him the girl's mother and father and His apostles He entered into the chamber wherein the girl was lying. There she lay, beautiful with the freshness of youth, disposed in form and figure, organized for life, so close to life, yet but a body and dead. There were eyes but they could not see, ears but they heard nothing, lips but no speech, a brain but no mind, no thought, no love, hands that could not touch or feel, feet that could not walk; there was blood but it did not flow, there was no pulse, no heartbeat. And Jesus took the girl by the hand and said to her: "Maid, arise." And that which was dead was living.

There was a brain and now also a mind and will, thought and love. The eyes had vision and they saw Christ, the ears heard His word, the lips spoke. She took the hand of Jesus in her own; she rose and walked and she was hungry.

Man without grace is as dead. There is a brain and a mind but God is not known. There is a will but it does not love God. There is strength but it can build only in time and for time, and with time the building crumbles. Man is small and knows his smallness but cannot acknowledge Him who alone is immense. Man is in need and knows his privation, yet knows not whom to ask for help nor how. Man has sinned and knows his sinning, but not the way to pardon.

God takes man and says to him: *Arise;* and the love of God brings forth grace. What was dead is living. The world of God opens to the mind, the goodness of God is within reach of the will. The weakness of man is strengthened by the omnipotence of God. Man knows that he is creature but he knows too that he is created out of love. He knows his need but knows also that he is the object of God's mercy, God's providence, God's care. He knows that he has sinned and that the Son of God has repaired that sin. He is grateful and in his gratitude he may offer God to God, Son to Father. By grace man has burst forth into life, a new life, a divine life transcending time, beyond this world. His every deed, his every thought, his every love has now an eternal echo, everlasting fruitfulness. In grace and by grace he speaks of God and to God; he knows His voice, walks with Him, and breathes the air of eternity. His whole being pulses with divinity and he is hungry; hungry to be perfect as the heavenly Father is perfect, to be dissolved and to be with Christ.

Grace is life and a new dimension to living, an expansion unto divine life. It breathes of beauty as a flower in the midst of a desert and the beauty is the beauty of God. It breathes of freedom as the flight of a bird seen through the bars of a prison and the freedom is the freedom of God. It breathes the love of friendship as a friend to one empty in loneliness; and the Friend by grace is God. It releases from earth into the world of angels. It unites with God, and through God with all, and by love.

48

Grace is love and the fruit of love; grace is life and life everlasting. In and by her Immaculate Conception this love, this life, was Mary's and in a plenitude beyond all men, all angels. Apart from that grace and its perfection, Mary has no life; and so it is that her grace, her Immaculate Conception, is her very definition, making her to be what she is, making her to be Mary.

The Immaculate Conception and Redemption

Grace is the love and life of God. Nature reflects God's love and life, for it is of His making. So we liken to Mary all of nature's greatest beauties, striving thereby to catch a glimpse of hers. She is the rose of patience, the lily of purity, the dove of peace, the garden enclosed in the love of God. Nature reflects God but man is God's image. The works of the art of man, the deeds of the life of man, in being of God's image, mirror God all the more perfectly. So we would honor Mary's grace in calling her the very temple and tabernacle of God fashioned by His love; she is the "army set in battle array" against all evil; she is the new Sion, the new Jerusalem, chosen by God and erected to His glory. Nature reflects God, man is His image. Jesus is the Son of God and God's revelation of Himself. He is the love and life of God and through Him can we attain most perfect insight into Mary. Her Immaculate Conception is because of Him.

To restore the gifts of God to man the Son of God was made man. To reopen the soul of man to the torrent of divine love Christ was conceived. To make satisfaction for man's sin, to convert man's punishment into the way to heaven, to lead men by that way, Christ was priest and victim, prophet and king. "God," says St. John, "did not send His Son into the world in order to judge the world, but that the world might be saved through Him." [6] As His passion began, Jesus said: "This is why I have come into the world." [7]

So from the first instant of His conception He gave to God what man by sinning had refused: the complete and perfect subjection of His human will to the will of the heavenly Father. St. Paul makes it most clear:

> Therefore in coming into the world, He says: Sacrifice and oblation Thou wouldst not, but a body Thou hast fitted to Me: In holocausts and sin-offerings Thou hast had no pleasure. Then said I: Behold, I come—in the head of the book it is written of Me—to do Thy will, O God. [8]

This is the inescapable theme of the life of Christ: "To do Thy will, O God." It is not an isolated act with which His life begins. It is the continuing, persevering motive of His living. "Amen, amen, I say to you, the Son can do nothing of Himself, but only what He sees the Father doing. For whatever He does, this the Son also does in like manner . . . Of myself I can do nothing . . . because I seek not my own will but the will of Him who sent Me." [9] The will of the Father is the very nourishment of His life: "My food is to do the will of Him who sent Me, to accomplish His work." [10]

On Calvary He completes His immolation, perfects His priesthood. That completion, that perfection consisted in this: He executed every decree of the will of God. Only when He had looked down the ages and consulted every prophecy, only when He knew that "all things were now accomplished that the Scripture might be fulfilled," only then did He say: *It is consummated,* and bowing His head, give up His spirit.[11]

Once God had cursed Lucifer and given promise to mankind: "I will put enmities between thee and the woman, between thy seed and her seed; he shall crush thy head and thou shalt lie in wait for his heel." [12] Mary was the promised woman and her Son hung upon the Cross. Lucifer is crushed and man is rescued from his domination. The Kingdom of God is restored. For that was Jesus born, for that He died. He hung upon the Cross, He shed His blood, He gave up His spirit to regain for men the kingdom lost. He ransomed what disobedience had forfeited; bought by humiliation what pride had spurned. He gained it again for the Adam who by sin had turned man from it, and for the child born this moment in Adam's sin. He hung upon the Cross and gained it for Mary.

He died that all men might be free of sin; He died that Mary might never know its slightest stain. He died that all men might live by grace and breathe of the Spirit of God; He died that Mary might be filled with grace and be overshadowed by God's Spirit, caught up in Him. He died that men might know God and knowing Him, love Him; He died that Mary might hold Him in her womb, beneath her heart, within her arms. He died that all men might be of the Kingdom of God; He died that Mary might be that Kingdom's Queen.

The Immaculate Conception shines luminous by contrast with the desolation wrought by sin. In being grace, the Immaculate Conception draws its meaning from the love and life of God. Christ is that God, and the cause of Mary and of Mary's every gift. They know Mary best who best know Christ.

There are those who criticize the Church for its devotion to Mary as derogating from the honor due to God, the honor due to Christ. We have all made answer with denials, distinctions and explanations. Yet we have wondered how they could be so blind. In our devotion to Mary we may have a problem but, if anything, it is opposed to this.

Catholic devotion to Mary neither distracts from God nor detracts from Christ. Quite the opposite is true and in the Immaculate Conception this truth is most manifest. The Immaculate Conception of Mary is "a singular grace and privilege of God Omnipotent" and gives glory to Him. The Immaculate Conception of Mary is of "the merits of Jesus Christ the Savior of the human race"; and in her Christ achieves His greatest victory.

Rather can Mary herself be hidden, become removed, even strange, as the creature moulded to undreamed perfection by the love of God and the passion of Christ. The Catholic never turns to Mary and in so doing turns aside from God or Christ. The Catholic may, however, find Mary remote in being so entirely filled with God and her divine Son. There is no difficulty in praising her as of the heaven of God, opened by Christ. But is she of earth, of this earth we know, of this world in which we live?

In making answer recourse may be had all too easily to sentimental imaginings. A vision of Mary in a daily round of household duties, cooking, sewing, washing, would be offered to render her human. Yet a haunting suspicion remains that this does not so much reveal as falsify.

Rather turn again to her Immaculate Conception.

Therein we see what God has made of Mary. Therein also do we see what God would make of man. The life of Mary in God, of God in Mary, is the will of God for men fulfilled most perfectly. She is the mirror reflective not only of God's eternal attributes but of His love of man and the perfection that love would create. No stain of sin obscures in her what God has prepared for those He loves. Mary is human with the fullness of the life that the creator and redeemer of human nature would pour out upon humanity. Mary is strange only in the measure that we have accepted an idea of man strange to the creator and redeemer of mankind. Mary is remote from us only in the measure that we are remote from God.

Why is Mary strange, remote from us? Why does it so easily appear to us that God made two worlds: the one, our own, filled with strife and struggle, with pride and hate and envy; the other, Mary, noble and serene, of untarnished purity?

Mary is strange by the singularity of her prerogatives, the uniqueness of her privileges. She is a woman set apart. Yet a little thought reveals this singularity of Mary to be, not an obstacle, but the very lever by which to understand and appreciate the dignity of man. The true greatness of a mountain is not measured by a hillock; it lies in being mentioned in the same breath with other, greater mountains. The uniqueness of the sun did not condemn men to live in darkness apart from it; it inspired them to bring forth light. The sublimity attained by Mary is clearest proof of the heights to which men have been called. The shining sanctity of Mary is a beacon to human aspirations. The singularity of Mary is of the hand of God stretched forth to all and indeed through Mary. By her prerogatives and gifts we know the generosity of God. So Mary's uniqueness does not beget despair but is the very measure of hope and what is hoped for.

In this does Mary set herself against the pride which first brought forth sin and against the very terms of pride's temptation. "Eat of the fruit and you shall be as gods" was Satan's invitation.[13] To be supreme and measure of all things has remained down through the ages man's most seductive yearning. It remained for our own time to erect a philosophy of life and of reality upon man's false and ever tottering supremacy. What has this made of man? To be supreme he must count himself among the animals or among the atoms and take his pride in that, for the moment, he is their most mysterious expression. By and in Mary, having part with her, man is numbered with the angels. Mary beckons us not to be as gods but as God Himself, to be the fullness of His image.

Mary seems nevertheless remote from the daily life that is our lot. We have no difficulty seeing God or Christ in her; we cannot see aught else. By God and the Son of God is she moulded, shaped and formed. Her life does not appear as ours to be a struggle to a goal, but rather to emerge, unfold unto a climax. Most clearly is this manifest in her Immaculate Conception. At the instant she begins to be she is most holy, possessed of God and to a surpassing degree. Here is no struggle with evil but evil warded off; no fight with sin's temptation but sin prevented.

Here again we must take thought. God is not only the end of all; He is for all the beginning. He is the fount and source of all that is and every good. Man comes forth from His creative hand; man continues to be by the continued will of that creative act; and the beginning of man's return to God and the perseverance of that journey is not of man but of God. By the grace of God is the first step taken and every step thereafter. There can be no ending in God save of that which begins in Him.

This is our lot: to take from God beginning and to unfold beneath His hand. "No one is good," said Christ, "but God." [14] There is in us no goodness, no life except as there is God in us; our goodness and our life are of His forming, shaping, moulding. We are alive as we are holy, and sanctity is the work of God. So the saints turn to God as beginning and begin to possess God as the end. Whatever is done apart from God is not our lot nor does it constitute our living; it is not life but death, and we were made to live.

Therein is contained the paradox at once of creation and of redemption. For creation it is the law of dependence, the law of providence: the greater the dependence upon God, the greater the influx of divine action. The result is the greater richness of being and goodness in the creature. For redemption it is the law of perfection, since to be perfect is to be entirely emptied of self and to belong entirely to God. So St. Paul could say: "As dying and behold we live." [15] Most briefly it is the law of grace, for by grace we live, and grace comes only from the loving will of God. So could the life of the saint be contained in the prayer: "O God, let me let You love me as You will."

It is no accident that materialism and naturalism, whether of Greek or modern age, stripped reality of its being and its goodness simply by casting it adrift from God. Without beginning in God it has no end, no goal, no purpose and dissolves into meaninglessness. In such a world man's vaunted independence finds only a closing, no fulfillment;

and he is left alone and friendless in a cold and alien universe. In such a world no goal can be presented worthy of the act of man, no purpose equal man's capacity. So action itself is glorified, and seeking is justified by seeking, not by what is sought. Not what is done but doing, not well or badly but in the exercise of freedom—by this there would be remedied the poverty-stricken emptiness of a world without a God.

The resultant life is neither life nor human but a horribly distorted caricature of both. In the Immaculate Conception is life in all its richness, human living to the full, for it begins and ends in God. Human freedom finds its meaning and its value in the liberty to choose and have the best. Human life is not made human by evil shared but evil conquered. To err is human but humanity is not defined by error; to sin is human but to live in sin is not to live as man. Freed of sin, Mary is not the weaker but the stronger in the fight; and the war she wages with Satan is the war of God and for the souls of men. In the battle with temptation she is from the beginning the leader giving strength, begetting courage. She was never subject to Satan and from her we know we need not be. In her we know our lot; with her we cast our lot with God.

That lot, that destiny, is mysterious for it is God and God is mystery. Yet that mystery is not totally unknown. God has revealed Himself in Christ and in Mary. In Christ we know the loving will of God for man; in Mary we see that will fulfilled. Theologians adduce many reasons for the fittingness of Mary' Immaculate Conception, and the basis of them all is her vocation. She is called to be the spouse of the Spirit of God; so it is not possible that even for an instant she be not His. She is called to be the Mother of the Son of God; so her purity must be as God the Father's, who also calls Him Son. She is called to be with Christ the conquerer of Satan; so never can she be under Satan's sway. All grace comes to men through her through whom comes Christ; and grace can have no part with sin. Queen of the sinless angels she will be for all eternity and in nowise can she be less, but always infinitely more, than they.

These reasons do not merely satisfy the human mind that Mary's first grace is a credible largess of God. They are the exposition of the fertility of that grace. All the glories of Mary, all her majestic privileges, are the unfolding, the radiation of the Immaculate Conception. By that Conception she is holy; by the grace of that Conception she grows to the fullness of sanctity. By that grace she is forever virgin; by that grace she consents to the angel; from that grace she draws the strength and generosity to stand beside the Cross and offer Christ and with Him give herself. By that grace fructified she showers graces on mankind; by that grace glorified she reigns as Queen.

The Immaculate Conception is not only an invitation to begin our life with God but a revelation of the wealth contained in that beginning. The predestination of Mary is the sign and measure of our predestination. Too often we recoil from the very term *predestination* as if it were an encroachment on our liberty or synonymous with doom. In truth, and in Mary the truth is clear and unequivocal, it is liberty's release and pledge of glory.

As in Mary so in us, by grace the Trinity indwells, we possess the goods of God, partake of God's own happiness. Why is this so and how? Because in Mary and in us, by grace is brought forth Christ. To bring forth Christ, in that does the Immaculate Conception consist. By the Immaculate Conception the Christ who is to be born *of* Mary is born *in* Mary. He fills her human nature with Himself as one day He will fill the nature that makes true man of Him. By the Divine Maternity He is hers; by the Immaculate Conception she is His. He absorbs and permeates her life with His. Yet what else is this but our vocation? our predestination? "Put on the Lord Jesus Christ," cries out St. Paul.[16] We are called to have the mind, the soul of Christ and by His Spirit to "search all things, even the deep things of God." [17]

Therein is answered too one lingering concern with strangeness, this time occasioned not by God's largess but its restraint. In freeing Mary of Adam's fault why did not God restore her to the unruffled joy and pleasure of Eden? Why did the grace of the Immaculate Conception contain the strength to bear with pain and sorrow rather than exempt from them? The answer lies plainly in the Christ brought forth. To Him was fitted a body capable of pain, not as a penalty for sin, but to bear sin's deserved punishment for all; so too in Mary. By her Immaculate Conception Mary was destined to be the new Eve, with Christ the new Adam, not in a paradise of earth, but on Calvary and in the eternal paradise of heaven.

The Immaculate Conception is a mystery of faith. All the exercise of the human mind does not make it less a mystery nor less of faith. For all the reasons adduced by theologians to render it credible, it is just that, credible— to be believed. But theology is not merely apologetic in intent, clenching its fist in self-defense; it would extend the fingers of the mind of man into the mind of God and partake of wisdom. Then is theology most childlike and the theologian most ready in his helplessness to be lifted up by God. Then mystery illumines mystery in the loving knowledge of the Holy Ghost.

Mary, and precisely in her Immaculate Conception, is the challenge laid down to us by God, the challenge to face the supernatural life in its full reality, in all the richness of its meaning, in all the grandeur of its vitality. She is the truth of God made manifest in the created order, and so simply by being Mary she is the answer to every heresy, to every truncation, compromise, adulteration of God's will for men. If we do not know her in her fullness, do not love her in her sublimity, do not imitate and take her to ourselves, the fault lies, not in her, but in our unwillingness to see, in our unwillingness to give ourselves to God.

In no other pure creature as in Mary does grace stand forth so clearly as the love of God and life in Him. In no other human person is the gulf by which sin separates from God revealed to be so deep, the least relic of sin so antagonistic to God's purity. Mary stands before us wholly supernaturalized in Christ. Not one act or some few deeds but her very being breathes the mystery of God's love. Without faith there is no life of Mary to behold. In the vision of faith she is the "woman clothed with the sun." [18] Truly could she testify: "He that is mighty has done great things to me. My soul does magnify the Lord." [19]

NOTES

[1] Translation taken from R. Garrigou-Lagrange, O.P., *The Mother of the Saviour* (Dublin, Standard House, 1940) p. 51.

[2] 2 Cor 5:15.

[3] Gen 1:26.

[4] Rom 5:12.

[5] Matth 9:23; Mark 5:38; Luke 8:51.

[6] John 3:17; cp. 12:47.

[7] John 18:37.

[8] Hebr 10:5.

[9] John 5:19, 30.

[10] John 4:34.

[11] John 19:30.

[12] Gen 3:15.

[13] Gen 3:5.

[14] Luke 18:19.

[15] 2 Cor 6:9.

[16] Rom 13:14.

[17] 1 Cor 2:10, 16.

[18] Apoc 12:1.

[19] Luke 1:46, 49.

The Assumption

VERY REVEREND MONSIGNOR GEORGE W. SHEA
IMMACULATE CONCEPTION SEMINARY
DARLINGTON, NEW JERSEY

The Assumption

Of the Encyclical, *Humani generis,* it has been remarked that, as in a Homeric poem, the very first words strike the keynote. That statement applies with even greater justice to our two most precious papal documents on the Blessed Mother.

The first of these, the Apostolic Letter whereby Pope Pius IX, just a century ago, solemnly defined the Virgin Mary's Immaculate Conception, begins with the words, "God Ineffable" (*"Ineffabilis Deus"*). And a similar phrase, "God Most Bountiful" (*"Munificentissimus Deus"*), ushers in the Apostolic Constitution of four years ago, wherein Pope Pius XII, gloriously reigning, solemnly defined Our Lady's bodily Assumption into heaven.

"God ineffable," "God most bountiful"—it would be difficult, if not impossible, to find a more appropriate introduction for either of these pontifical documents. Exalted tributes they are indeed to that fairest and choicest of mere creatures, Mary; but at the same time and above all, both papal bulls render a yet higher homage, to God Himself, the Author of Our Lady's supernatural perfections.

The glory of the holy and undivided Trinity is cited by each as the ultimate motive for their respective dogmatic definitions, that of the Immaculate Conception and that of the Assumption.[1] Moreover, both Sovereign Pontiffs set forth Mary's singular privileges precisely as effects and manifestations of God's boundless mercy, wisdom, providence and power.

Thus, in the sublime initial paragraphs of *Ineffabilis Deus*, Pius IX declares how the almighty, all-wise and merciful God, foreseeing the fall of Adam and the resultant wretchedness of the entire human race, in His providence decreed the Incarnation of the Word, in order that man, who had been led into sin by the cunning of Satan, would not perish; and in order that what had been lost in the first Adam would be gloriously restored by the Second Adam.

Accordingly, Pius IX continues, from the very beginning and before all time, the eternal Father selected and prepared for His only-begotten Son a Mother of whom He would be made flesh. And upon her God lavished a singular love, pouring forth an abundance of heavenly gifts so that she, ever incomparably holy and free even from the least taint of original sin, would be a fitting Mother for the Son of God and, as a new Eve, would (together with the new Adam) triumph completely over the ancient serpent.[2]

In short, as the same Sovereign Pontiff states soon thereafter, the origin of the Blessed Virgin was foreordained by God in precisely the same decree as the Incarnation of the Divine Word.[3]

This predestined dignity of Mary as the Mother of the Divine Redeemer was the reason why God decreed also to shower upon her those many other supernatural privileges and prerogatives which exalt her above all the angels and all the saints. As Pope Pius XII came to say in a key passage of *Munificentissimus Deus*:

> Hence the revered Mother of God, from all eternity joined in a hidden way with Jesus Christ in one and the same decree of predestination [—*Ineffabilis Deus*], immaculate in her conception, a most perfect virgin in her divine motherhood, the noble associate of the divine Redeemer who has won a complete triumph over sin and its consequences, was finally granted, as the supreme culmination of her privileges, that she should be preserved free from the corruption of the tomb and that, like her own Son, having overcome death, she might be taken up body and soul to the glory of heaven where, as Queen, she sits in splendor at the right hand of her Son, the immortal King of the Ages.[4]

Thus the Pope of the Assumption. We have quoted from him and from the Pope of the Immaculate Conception for a twofold reason. For one thing, these pontiffs exhibit Catholic Marian devotion in its proper perspective, as entirely subordinated to and in the service of devotion to God—therefore, as something far removed from that Mariolatry of which we are often accused.

At the same time, the cited passages furnish us with an invaluable compendium of Mariology. For, in unfolding the Blessed Mother's special role in the drama of salvation, they disclose the inner coherence of Marian doctrines one with another and with the rest of Revelation. Therewith is had an excellent, if somewhat lengthy, introduction to the present paper, which will discuss Our Lady's bodily Assumption, first, as considered in itself; then, as considered in relation to the rest of Mariology and to theology as a whole. A fourth and final phase of our paper will dwell on *Maria Assumpta* in relation to the modern world, her providential significance for our times.

Since Nov. 1, 1950, any study of Our Lady's bodily Assumption into heavenly glory must, of course, base itself on the Apostolic Constitution, *Munificentissimus Deus,* especially the solemn dogmatic definition of the doctrine, which is found near the close of the bull. Only in that definition is Pope Pius XII speaking *ex cathedra,* exercising his supreme teaching authority. However, that is not to say that the earlier part of the bull, which recounts the history of and the grounds for Catholic belief in the Assumption, is without weight or value. For there the Holy Father is exercising his ordinary teaching authority,[5] and those earlier words of his shed much light on the definition itself.

In the interest of brevity we must be content to give the Pope's own lucid summary of that historico-doctrinal exposition, before we come to the definition itself. The summary reads:

> Since the Universal Church, within which dwells the Spirit of Truth Who infallibly directs it toward an ever more perfect knowledge of the revealed truths, has expressed its own belief many times over the course of the centuries, and since the Bishops of the entire world have almost unanimously petitioned that the truth of the bodily Assumption of the Blessed Virgin Mary into heaven should be defined as a dogma of

divine and Catholic faith—this truth which is based on the Sacred Writings, which is thoroughly rooted in the minds of the faithful, which has been approved in ecclesiastical worship from the most remote times, which is completely in harmony with the other revealed truths, and which has been expounded and explained magnificently in the work, the science, and the wisdom of the theologians—We believe that the moment appointed in the plan of divine providence for the solemn proclamation of this outstanding privilege of the Virgin Mary has already arrived.[6]

Then, having first enlarged upon the opportuneness, the providential aspects of a solemn proclamation of the Assumption precisely in this crucial stage of human history, the Vicar of Christ proceeds to the formal definition itself, which reads:

We pronounce, declare, and define it to be a divinely revealed dogma: that the Immaculate Mother of God, the ever Virgin Mary, having completed the course of her earthly life, was assumed body and soul into heavenly glory.[7]

This *ex cathedra* pronouncement, it should be noted, defines not one but two things. For it embraces not only the doctrine of Our Lady's glorious Assumption in body and soul but also the fact that the doctrine is a divinely revealed dogma: that is, a truth contained in the deposit of divine public revelation (hence, in Sacred Scripture and/or Tradition) and which, after proposition by the Church, must be believed with the assent of divine and

Catholic faith.[8] In other words, we have here a "dogmatic" definition.

The Holy Father's declaration that the doctrine of the Assumption is a divinely revealed dogma will occupy our attention later on. Our immediate interest centers on the dogma itself, on the precise meaning of the Assumption as dogmatically defined by Pope Pius XII.

To be sure, the general sense of the Holy Father's words is unmistakable. Our Lady was exempted from that law which holds for the rank and file of humans when their earthly exile is over. In virtue of that general law, the just, though their souls may already have attained heaven, must wait until the end of time for full victory over death, for their bodies to be joined each to its own glorious soul.[9]

But with Mary it was otherwise. The immaculate and virginal Mother of God was not subject to the law of remaining in the corruption of the grave; she did not have to wait until the Last Day for the redemption of her body.[10] For she was taken up into the glory of heaven soul and body. Soon, if not immediately, after the conclusion of her earthly pilgrimage she was granted that consummation of her existence which we mean when we confess, as our own hope, "the resurrection of the body and life everlasting." For Mary, the Last Day, insofar as it means the resurrection and glorification of the bodies of the just, has been wonderfully anticipated. Briefly, Our Lady's lot after this earthly exile was the privileged one of a total glorification.

So much for the general import of the Blessed Virgin's Assumption as dogmatically defined by Pope Pius XII. However, there is much more to the definition than meets

70

the eye. Therefore, we shall try to unfold and circumscribe its meaning somewhat more accurately.

To begin with, let us recall these words of the formal definition: *"the Immaculate Mother of God, the ever Virgin Mary,* having completed the course of her earthly life, was assumed body and soul into heavenly glory." Thus the subject of the definition is Mary herself, in her entirety; therefore, her very person, which is constituted by the vital union of her soul and body. To quote St. Bonaventure, "the soul is not a person, but the soul, joined to the body, is a person." [11]

At first glance, then, the Pope's language would seem to say that the very person of Mary was assumed all at once and precisely as such, as person, as incarnate spirit. In that case, Our Lady's total glorification, i.e. her glorification in body as well as in soul, would have been total from the start, would have been accomplished immediately rather than in stages. Her body would have entered into heavenly glory simultaneously with her soul.

If such really is the Pope's meaning, then one would have to conclude that the Blessed Mother did not die. For it is at least theologically certain that, so soon as her earthly pilgrimage terminated, her utterly sinless soul was straightway admitted to the beatific vision, straightway glorified. Hence, if Mary's body was glorified simultaneously with her soul, this would rule out death, that is, any separation of body and soul even for an instant.

But does the Holy Father actually teach as much, thus vindicating those few theologians who hold that at the end of her earthly exile, Mary was taken up into heavenly glory at once, without first undergoing death? In other words, does the Pope actually reject the view of the overwhelming majority of theologians, who maintain that Our Lady's bodily Assumption into heavenly glory was preceded by death, by the immediate glorification of her soul, and by the glorious resurrection of her body?

In answer to these questions we firmly state that Pius XII in no wise wished to exclude the latter theory, the much more common opinion, the view that Mary's glorification was indeed total, but not immediately so. In declaring that the Immaculate Mother of God, the ever Virgin Mary, was assumed into heavenly glory, the Pope wished rather to rule out any thought that Our Lady's body, assumed into heaven, is separated from her soul. That is to say, excluded is anything like the double Assumption theory found in some ancient apocryphal writers, according to whom the Virgin Mary's soul was taken up into heaven but her body was transported to some terrestrial paradise, there to be preserved from corruption until resurrection on the Last Day. Incidentally, such notions are further precluded by the fact that the Pope says Our Lady's body was assumed *into heavenly glory*. The celestial glorification of a body presupposes and derives from its union with a glorified soul.

To return to the controversial question of Mary's death, an objective analysis of *Munificentissimus Deus* will reveal that, neither in the formal definition, nor anywhere else in the bull, does the Sovereign Pontiff commit himself on this subject. He remains neutral throughout. In the formal definition he deliberately uses the non-committal expression, "having completed the course of her earthly life." The same reticence is observable elsewhere, whenever the Pope is speaking in his own person. In other passages, where Church Fathers and theologians are let speak, a certain number of texts do give one to understand that Mary died, but these quotations are adduced by the Holy Father only to put in bold relief the incorruption of the Blessed Mother's virginal body.

So, then, the debate about Our Lady's bodily mortality may and does continue. The controversy is too involved to be gone into here. Suffice it to say that the thesis of Mary's death is the much more common and much more probable doctrine. It can claim the support of Pope Pius XI, who, in an allocution, after urging prayer to Mary assumed into heavenly glory, added that the Blessed Mother died, since she possessed "not the grace of creation but rather the grace of redemption, which did not confer immortality truly and properly so called." [12]

In the hypothesis of Our Lady's death one can go on to ask how long a period elapsed between it and her glorious resurrection and bodily Assumption. Needless to say, no matter how long that interval may have been, in the interim Mary's virginal body was in no wise subject to decay. For, her preservation from all corruption of the tomb is Catholic doctrine which pervades the historico-doctrinal portion of *Munificentissimus Deus*. As to the length of the interval between the Blessed Mother's death and resurrection, theologians can only speculate. Their theories range from a single moment, to minutes or hours or, at most, a few days. This last is the limit imposed by the formal definition in *Munificentissimus Deus,* since its language clearly intimates that Mary's bodily Assumption occurred fairly soon, if not immediately, after the completion of her earthly life. For this reason, not to mention many others, one must reject the well-meant proposal of an Anglican divine, Dr. B. Mascall, who suggested that

Our Lady's resurrection and Assumption may have come to pass "three or four hundred years after her death." [13]

Continuing our analysis of the solemn definition of the Assumption, we now turn to its final phrase, "into heavenly glory." Since the Holy Father says nothing about the nature of this "heavenly glory," obviously he is content to have it understood in the light of traditional Catholic doctrine on the subject.

According to that doctrine, total celestial glorification consists in the supernatural beatitude of the soul, which results from the intuitive vision of God, and which in turn effects a preternatural transformation of the body. One could pause here to point out that, in view of the supernatural and preternatural elements it involves, Our Lady's glorious Assumption is something which could not be known naturally. However, it is more convenient to develop this important topic later on. At present our interest centers rather on two of the preternatural qualities of a glorified body, and on their implications for Mary's Assumption.

These qualities are the gift of impassibility, precluding all "pain and inconvenience of any sort," and the gift of agility, enabling the body to move "with the utmost facility and speed, wherever the soul wishes." [14] Thanks to these and to the other preternatural qualities of a glorified body, the latter is no longer subject to the physical laws of nature, as can be gathered from the Gospel accounts of the risen Christ. Consequently, even if Our Lady's Assumption did involve an ascent into the stratosphere or even beyond, one cannot legitimately invoke against our doctrine arguments drawn from the physical sciences. Absurd, therefore, was the objection raised, four years ago, by Dr. Anton J. Carlson, who was then president of the National Society for Medical Research, and Professor Emeritus of Physiology at the University of Chicago. The scientist argued that, if Mary did go "up through the atmosphere, . . . she would surely have died of asphyxia the moment she got up 50,000 feet." [15]

Incidentally, Dr. Carlson supposes it to be a dogma of our faith that heaven is located somewhere in outer space. Is this actually the case? Not at all. To begin with, note that, in dogmatically defining the Assumption, Pope Pius XII did not state that Our Lady's body was transferred from one place to another, from earth to heaven. While, as we shall say in a moment, the Marian privilege did involve such a change of place, that fact does not fall under the formal definition. The formal definition simply declares that Mary, "having completed the course of her earthly life, was assumed into heavenly glory (*ad caelestem gloriam assumptam*)." Not "into heaven," but "into heavenly glory." Defined, therefore, is this and no more: a change of Mary's state or condition, her transfer in body and soul from the condition of an earthly pilgrim to that of celestial glory.

There is good reason for this careful language in the formal definition. For it is not a dogma of faith that heaven, besides being a state or condition of beatitude, involves also some region or place inhabited by the blessed.[16] To be sure, this conception of heaven, though not a dogma of faith, is nevertheless the much more common opinion of theologians, one which has the support of several expressions used by Pius XII in the expository section of *Munificentissimus Deus*.

In all probability, then, Our Lady's bodily Assumption

did indeed involve a transfer of her body from earth to some heavenly abode. But just where that place is situated, no one can say. It is not necessarily off in the stratosphere somewhere, or even above the earth at all. If Sacred Scripture, the Creeds, and the Church Fathers seem to speak otherwise, as though heaven were definitely up in the sky, their language can be understood as mere accomodation to the mentality and cosmological notions of the times; from that language nothing certain can be gathered as to the location of heaven.[17]

For a final comment on the dogma defined in *Munificentissimus Deus,* we may remark that the formal definition does not term Our Lady's bodily Assumption a privilege. However, this aspect of the Blessed Virgin's final lot is obvious, and, in any event, is frequently affirmed in the historico-doctrinal part of *Munificentissimus Deus,* which, in fact, even refers to this Marian privilege as a singular one, a "singular triumph." [18]

This raises an interesting question. If Our Lady's privilege is called a singular one, must we then hold that, other than Christ, none but Mary has as yet been assumed bodily into heavenly glory?

Not necessarily. For one thing, whereas *Munificentissimus Deus* refers to the Blessed Mother's Immaculate Conception as an *entirely* singular privilege (*singulari prorsus privilegio*),[19] it never applies that restrictive qualification to the singular privilege of Mary's bodily Assumption. Moreover, in the two instances where he speaks of the divine law requiring the just to wait until the Last Day for the glorification of their bodies, the Holy Father terms this law a "general" one, rather than a universal one.[20]

76

Further, one must consider a celebrated passage of the First Gospel. In his account of Our Lord's Passion, St. Matthew declares (27:52–53) that "the tombs were opened, and many bodies of the saints who had fallen asleep arose; and coming forth out of the tombs after His (Christ's) resurrection, they came into the holy city, and appeared to many."

There are many weighty reasons to suppose that this resurrection of the dead, which was subsequent rather than prior to Christ's own, was a definitive one, which was followed by the bodily assumption of those saints into heaven. "They formed the escort of the Conqueror of death in his triumphal entry into the abode of glory." [21] As a matter of fact, this was the almost unanimous interpretation of the Matthaean text throughout the first four or five centuries, as well as the firm view of many of the Church's most eminent theologians and exegetes from the Middle Ages on down to the present day.[22]

Far from detracting from the Marian privilege, the aforesaid interpretation of Matthew tends to lend credence to it in non-Catholic circles.[23] Indeed, from that interpretation one can develop a positive and, at bottom, scriptural argument in behalf of Our Lady's bodily Assumption. For, if Sacred Scripture attests that some have been vouchsafed total glorification before the Last Day, then surely the Immaculate and ever virginal Mother of God must have been similarly privileged. It is a solid Mariological principle that every supernatural and preternatural privilege which, on the testimony of Revelation, has been granted to another or others, must also have been given to that choicest and most beloved of God's creatures, Mary.[24]

To conclude this matter, note finally that, if others

besides the Blessed Virgin gained redemption of their bodies before the Last Day, Mary's privilege would still remain a "singular triumph," if only for the reason that she was spared the corruption of the tomb which had been the lot of those others before their glorious resurrection and assumption. Indeed, it would remain singular for the further reason that Mary's privilege rests on her incomparable role in the economy of salvation.[25]

Here ends our commentary on the doctrine of the Assumption as defined by Pope Pius XII. It is time to turn our attention to that other element of the formal definition, the Holy Father's declaration that the doctrine is a divinely revealed dogma. This means that the Assumption of Our Lady is a truth contained in the deposit of divine public Revelation, which closed with the death of the last Apostle; in other words, that it is a truth which God has conveyed to us by Sacred Scripture and/or Tradition, and which must be believed with the assent of divine faith, an assent whose motive is the authority of God revealing—God, who can neither deceive nor be deceived.

The Holy Father's pronouncement that the Marian privilege is a divinely revealed dogma is noteworthy on several grounds. For one thing, it serves to emphasize that our belief in Mary's Assumption is not, as many non-Catholics contend, the product of fantastic myths and legends.

Further, the same pronouncement implies that this our belief is not based on mere historical testimonies, which would have originated from eyewitnesses of the Assumption. For, even if there had been eyewitnesses of Mary's privilege, theirs would be merely human testimonies, not

78

divine Revelation, not that testimony which alone can command the assent of divine faith—the testimony of God Himself.

As a matter of fact, in the final analysis there could not have been any human witnesses of Our Lady's Assumption into heavenly glory. Speaking of that privilege, *Munificentissimus Deus* expressly declares that "surely no faculty of the human mind could know (it) by its own natural powers, as far as the heavenly glorification of the virginal body of the revered Mother of God is concerned." [26]

In other words, Mary's bodily Assumption into heavenly glory is something outside the province of mere history; it is a "transhistoric" truth, a supernatural mystery, something knowable only from divine Revelation. For, as we have already seen, celestial glorification embraces the supernatural beatitude of the soul, deriving from the intuitive vision of God, and the resultant preternatural transformation of the body, matters which cannot be perceived by our senses and hence cannot be known by the natural powers of our intellect.[27] According to St. Thomas Aquinas, the visibility of a glorified body to earthly eyes depends entirely upon the will of the glorified person. But even if the latter does choose to manifest himself, the fact of his glorification remains unperceived by the senses. The same St. Thomas has pointed out that even in the case of Our Lord's Ascension, which may be taken as the exemplar of Our Lady's Assumption, an angel came to the witnesses who were present on that occasion and formally revealed to them whither Jesus had gone.[28]

To sum up, not only is the Assumption of truth known from divine Revelation, it is a truth which could not have become known in any other way.

And, of course, the Revelation by which it became known is public Revelation, which terminated with the death of the last Apostle, St. John. For, truths subsequently communicated, by private revelations, are not part of our Catholic faith, and cannot be declared a divinely revealed dogma, as Pope Pius XII did declare the doctrine of Our Lady's Assumption. Worth mentioning here is the Holy Father's express quotation of the Vatican Council's teaching that "the Holy Ghost was not promised to the successors of Peter in such a way that, by His revelation, they might manifest new doctrine, but so that, by His assistance, they might guard as sacred and might faithfully propose the revelation delivered through the Apostles, or the deposit of faith." [29] In error, therefore, was Graham Greene's article in *Life* magazine, four years ago (Oct. 30, 1950), insofar as it tended to suggest that Catholic belief in the Assumption rests on private revelations and apparitions.

Not only is such a supposition erroneous but, we may add by way of transition to the next stage of our paper, it betrays a surprising underestimation of the importance of the doctrine of the Assumption. For the latter is not some minor truth which, if it rated revelation at all, could have been left to private revelation; a truth having no necessary connection with the Christian scheme of salvation; a truth which could be denied without prejudice to fundamental tenets of the Christian faith.[30]

On the contrary, this privilege of Our Lady is an integral part of an interlocking whole; it is intimately interwoven with other Mariological truths, and, like them, with yet other Catholic doctrines. *Munificentissimus Deus* speaks often of the wonderful harmony and order of the gifts which God has lavished upon Mary, of the marvelous accord between her Assumption and her other prerogatives, of which the former is the "supreme culmination." [31] Writing in the sixteenth century, Suarez, the great Jesuit theologian, noted the primordial importance always attached to the feast of the Assumption. "It is," he declared, "in some sort the feast that is proper to the holy Virgin. Among all her feasts it has a quite special excellence, because it presents to us the glory, the reward and the triumph of the all holy Virgin." [32] In short, Our Lady's Assumption is, as it were, a recapitulation of all her other privileges.

So manifold are the interrelations of this doctrine with the rest of Mariology and with other areas of theology, that only the more notable ones can be traced here. For a point of departure the formal definition of the dogma will serve admirably. As has been said, the Holy Father declared that "the Immaculate Mother of God, the ever Virgin Mary, having completed the course of her earthly life, was assumed body and soul into heavenly glory."

"The Immaculate Mother of God, the ever Virgin Mary . . ." Therewith are indicated the three other solemnly defined Marian dogmas: Our Lady's divine maternity, her perpetual virginity, and her Immaculate Conception. Although the Sovereign Pontiff is not here defining that the Assumption is connected with and flows from those other privileges, as a matter of fact the latter furnish theologians with three of their main arguments for the total glorification of Our Lady; and, moreover, they appear in the Pope's own summary of grounds for the Assumption. That summary has been quoted above, but we must repeat it here:

Hence the revered Mother of God, from all eternity joined in a hidden way with Jesus Christ in one and the same decree of predestination, immaculate in her conception, a most perfect virgin in her divine motherhood, the noble associate of the divine Redeemer who has won a complete triumph over sin and its consequences, was finally granted, as the supreme culmination of her privileges, that she should be preserved free from the corruption of the tomb and that, like her own Son, having overcome death, she might be taken up body and soul to the glory of heaven where, as Queen, she sits in splendor at the right hand of her Son, the immortal King of the Ages.[33]

In this papal catalogue of doctrinal "considerations" supporting the truth of the Assumption, reference is made not only to the three Marian privileges previously mentioned, but to two others as well, the Blessed Mother's noble association with her divine Son in the work of redemption, and her queenship. Doubtless, these two prerogatives were not mentioned in the formal definition because they are not yet solemnly defined dogmas of our faith. Nevertheless, they too provide powerful arguments for the total glorification of Our Lady. In fact, the most decisive argument of all is that which is contained in the truth that Mary was the intimate associate of the divine Saviour in His redemptive task. As will be learned in due course, this is the doctrinal consideration most emphasized by the Pope himself. Hence we shall first concentrate on it before returning to the other arguments.

It is Catholic doctrine that the Blessed Mother was associated with her divine Son in accomplishing the salvation of mankind. To cite but a few instances of papal teaching on this subject, Leo XIII declared that "the Immaculate Virgin (was) chosen to be the Mother of God and thereby associated with Him in the work of man's salvation." [34] Clearer still is the statement of Pope Pius XI, repeated by his successor in the recent encyclical on the Feast of Mary, Queen, to the effect that Our Lady was the beloved Mother of Christ precisely "so that she might be made His associate in the redemption of the human race." [35] One of the present Holy Father's several references to this doctrine, in *Munificentissimus Deus*, we have already noted in the passage given above, and another will be quoted soon.

The biblical basis for affirming Mary's association in the work of the Redemption is found in the Protoevangelium in Genesis 3:15—the Protogospel, those First Glad Tidings which God announced to mankind by way of this malediction pronounced upon Satan:

> I will put enmity between you and the woman,
> between your seed and her seed;
> he shall crush your head,
> and you shall lie in wait for his heel.[36]

The Mariological meaning of the Protoevangelium, that is, that the "woman" of Genesis 3:15 refers in some real sense to the Mother of the Redeemer, is indubitable, especially in the light of papal interpretations of the text. Accordingly, as can be verified by a detailed exegetical analysis of the Protoevangelium,[37] the latter predicts not only the work of the redemption by Christ, the sweeping victory of the Redeemer over sin and its consequences, but also Mary's intimate association in that work, her participation in that victory, in all its fulness.

This teaching of the Protoevangelium, which is paralleled by the ancient patristic doctrine on Our Lady as the New Eve,[38] is a treasury of Marian truths. From it theologians vindicate Our Lady's title of Coredemptrix, and her immunity from personal sin. Pope Pius IX employed it in behalf of Mary's immunity from original sin, her Immaculate Conception.[39] From the Protoevangelium Pope Pius XII derived an argument for Our Lady's queenship, in his recent encyclical on that subject.[40] And the same pontiff made the Protoevangelium the basis of what he evidently considers the foremost direct proof of the revealed character of the Blessed Mother's conquest of death, her bodily Assumption into heavenly glory. Here are his celebrated words in *Munificentissimus Deus:*

> We must remember especially that, since the second century, the Virgin Mary has been designated by the holy Fathers as the new Eve, who, although subject to the new Adam, is most intimately associated with Him in that struggle against the infernal foe which, as foretold in the Protoevangelium, finally resulted in that most complete victory over sin and death which are always mentioned together in the writings of the Apostle of the Gentiles (cf. Romans, 5–6; 1 Corinthians, 15:21–26, 54–57). Consequently, just as the glorious resurrection of Christ was an essential part and the final sign of this victory, so that struggle which was common to the Blessed Virgin and her divine Son should be brought to a close by the glorification of her virginal body, for the same Apostle says: 'when this mortal body puts on immortality, then shall come to pass the word that is

written: Death is swallowed up in victory!' (1 Corinthians, 15:54).[41]

Justly therefore does the Holy Father insist in *Munificentissimus Deus* that the doctrine of Our Lady's Assumption is based ultimately on Sacred Scripture.[42] The Marian privilege is formally implicitly revealed in the Protoevangelium coupled with the texts of St. Paul. It is contained, as a part in the whole, in the biblical doctrine of Our Lady's predestined role as the intimate associate of the Redeemer, a participant in His complete victory over sin and its consequences, one of which is the necessity of remaining in the toils of death. Without her glorious bodily Assumption, Mary's victory would not have been complete, any more than it would have been complete without her Immaculate Conception, or without her freedom from all personal sin, even venial, or without her virginal motherhood, which constitutes a victory over another consequence of sin, concupiscence. The Assumption is the crowning realization and fulfillment of the divine promise and prophecy which stands at the beginning of the Bible.

Truly, then, the total glorification of Our Lady is no minor, inconsequential doctrine, with but a tenuous relation to the rest of our Christian faith. However one may care to judge the arguments yet to come, the argument from the Woman of the Protoevangelium has firmly established the necessary connection of the Assumption with the divine economy of salvation, with God's plan of Redemption. And one may repeat this for what is essentially the same argument, the patristic doctrine of the New Eve.

As to those other arguments, mentioned some time ago, it must suffice to let them pass rapidly in review. One finds them employed again and again by the Church Fathers and Doctors and theologians quoted throughout *Munificentissimus Deus*. Thus, one favorite argument is to the effect that "Mary was assumed because she is the Mother of God." The reasoning runs that, by conceiving and giving birth to the God-man, Our Lady was endowed with an almost infinite dignity. Moreover, by her divine maternity she contracted not only a relationship of consanguinity with the Word Incarnate according to the flesh, but further, no less real, relationships—of affinity—with each of the three divine Persons, which introduced her, as it were, into the family of the Blessed Trinity. It is impossible to suppose, the argument continues, that so exalted a person could be indefinitely condemned to the state of death, especially since this would reflect on the honor and glory of the Blessed Trinity. And to these there is added the consideration that, beyond a shadow of a doubt, Jesus Christ has Himself observed, in a most perfect way, the divine commandment by which children are ordered to honor their parents.

As to the argument from Our Lady's virginity, it is formulated in various ways, of which the following is an example. It is a revealed truth that Mary remained a virgin even in giving birth to Jesus. Hence she was immune from the curse pronounced upon Eve in Genesis 3:16: "I will make great your distress in childbearing; in pain shall you bring forth children." Now, this particular curse is only one of the punishments inflicted because of original sin. Hence, if the Blessed Mother was immune from the one curse, it is logical to conclude that she was also immune from the corruption of the grave, which is but another aspect of the same general curse (Genesis 3:19; 3:3).

A further argument for Our Lady's bodily Assumption

is often drawn from her Immaculate Conception. That there is a close bond between the two has been emphasized by Pope Pius XII, in *Munificentissimus Deus*,[43] and again in *Fulgens Corona,* the Encyclical which promulgated the Marian Year. We may quote from the latter:

> And so these two very singular privileges, bestowed upon the Virgin Mother of God, stand out in most splendid light as the beginning and as the end of her earthly journey; for the greatest possible glorification of her virgin body is the complement, at once appropriate and marvelous, of the absolute innocence of her soul, which was free from all stain; and just as she took part in the struggle of her only-begotten Son with the wicked serpent of hell, so also she shared in His glorious triumph over sin and its sad consequences.[44]

However, this and the other papal passage may be interpreted to mean no more than the existence of an extrinsic connection between the Assumption and the Immaculate Conception. That is to say, without affirming that the former can be argued from the latter, the Holy Father simply points out that each privilege is rooted in Mary's role as Christ's associate and sharer in His complete victory over the devil, whence the Immaculate Conception and the Assumption can mutually illumine one another, as partial aspects of the complete victory.

Of course, this does not forbid theologians to assert an intrinsic or necessary connection between the Immaculate Conception and the Assumption; and, in fact, not a few do insist that Mary was assumed "because she was immaculate." They reason that, in virtue of her Immaculate Conception, Our Lady was completely removed from the atmosphere of fault, and therefore could not possibly incur any of the punishments for original sin, such as being subject to the dominion of death up to the time of the general resurrection. So, then, far from being merely a fitting complement to the Immaculate Conception, the Blessed Mother's glorious bodily Assumption was a necessary sequel to that other privilege.

Finally, we come to the argument from Our Lady's queenship. Although this royal dignity is not a solemnly defined dogma, still, it is an age-old Catholic belief, proposed by the universal ordinary magisterium of the Church, that Mary is the Queen of heaven and earth, reigning over all the angels and saints and the whole of mankind.[45] Now, one may reason, it is unthinkable that so noble a queen could be present in heaven only as spirit and not yet as incarnate spirit. For, first of all, the state of a separated soul is a violent one, utterly opposed to man's deepest tendencies; a state, moreover, which has been brought about by sin, and which deprives the human person of an essential part of his nature—leaving him at best an incomplete person, truncated, mutilated.

All this ill accords with the royal dignity of the Virgin Mary. She, incomplete in her own being, would be in the situation of having as her subjects beings perfect in their own proper nature—the angels, and very likely, those risen saints spoken of in Matthew 27:52–53, who in all probability were assumed into heavenly glory in body and soul. That would be an abnormal situation, since a Queen should not be in a state inferior to that of her subjects.

Further, the hypothesis that Our Lady was not assumed into heaven in body as well as soul would make for a shocking disparity between Christ, the King, and Mary, His Queen. While He reigns, resplendent in the glory of

His risen body, at His side would be His very own Mother, in a state of imperfection, deprived of that part of her being which was, in fact, a cause of His exaltation, since it was from her flesh that the Son of God was made man. In the light of these reflections, not to mention others which could be added, one may argue that Mary was assumed in soul and body "because she is Queen."

So much for a summary of arguments in behalf of Our Lady's bodily Assumption, insofar as they are drawn from her divine maternity, virginity, Immaculate Conception, and queenship. All theologians admit that each of these arguments is at least one of fittingness, displaying the eminent appropriateness of the bodily Assumption, and confirming the decisive argument from the Protoevangelium. Some go further and consider one or the other of the arguments to be apodictic, yielding the doctrine of the bodily Assumption as a logical conclusion from, a necessary corollary to, some other Marian privilege, in which Mary's total glorification would be contained either virtually, or even formally-implicitly.

Whatever may be the respective merits of these differing views,[46] it should not be overlooked that if the aforesaid arguments are taken, not separately, but together, from their convergence and their collective weight they should suffice to remove all hesitation in accepting Our Lady's bodily Assumption into heaven, even if we did not have the infallible pronouncement of *Munificentissimus Deus,* or the equally infallible teaching of the universal ordinary magisterium,[47] or the indubitably decisive argument from the Protoevangelium and the Patristic doctrine of the New Eve.

In any case, and this has been our chief purpose in unfolding them, the various arguments vindicate the Holy Father's assertion of a wonderful harmony and order existing among Mary's privileges, his insistence on the perfect accord between her Assumption and those other prerogatives, of which the former is the "supreme culmination."

In studying that harmony, order, and accord insofar as it sheds light on the Assumption, at the same time we gathered that the latter doctrine in its turn has enriched and illumined vast reaches of Mariology, deepening, for example, our understanding of the Blessed Mother's co-redemptive role, and of her queenship whereby she continues to exercise her universal mediation.[48] Since Mary is glorified in the full integrity of her nature, her queenly role, which is essentially maternal and mediatorial, is seen to be in its own degree something utterly perfect and a fitting parallel to that of her divine Son, Christ the King and supreme Mediator. If it be true that the body participates in some fashion in the acts of the soul, then Our Lady's presence in heaven as a complete person seems to confer on her mediation a singular propriety: for her corporal condition renders her not only more like to the risen and glorified Christ than are the separated souls in heaven, but also closer to men still on earth.

One is tempted to dwell longer on these new Mariological horizons opened up by the solemn definition of Our Lady's bodily Assumption into heavenly glory, but it still remains for us to suggest at least a few of the relations of our doctrine with other areas of theology, and also to discuss briefly the providential significance of *Maria Assumpta* for the modern world.

According to the well-known adage, of liturgical provenance,[49] that Mary has destroyed all heresies, Mariology is the touchstone of orthodoxy, the bulwark of other truths of our faith, especially of Catholic Christology. As the saying goes, he who believes rightly about Our Lady, believes rightly all along the line. Celebrated is the role of the Mother of God in rescuing us from the divided Christ of Nestorianism,[50] and the pallid Christ of Protestantism. To quote Coventry Patmore's line, she is "our only Savior from an abstract Christ."

One should realize, however, that besides confirming and defending the already explicit tenets of Catholicism, Marian truths shed additional light upon them, and make for further progress, stimulating theologians to deeper penetration and advances in their sacred science. The function of Mariology in relation to the development of doctrine has been likened to that of a photographer's developing reagent.

It goes without saying that these general statements about the contributions of Mariology to the conservation and explicitation of Catholic beliefs hold true in particular for the Assumption.

Indeed, so manifold are the contributions of this precious truth to theology in general, that they defy even a bare listing here. One must be content with the brief mention of but a few. To begin with, as the introduction and subsequent course of this paper have intimated, Our Lady's bodily Assumption confirms and exalts several divine attributes which are so widely denied today—God's all-wise providence, His mercy, bounty and power. Now more than ever can we appreciate Mary's own tribute to these divine perfections, in her inspired *Magnificat:* "He who is mighty has done great things for me. . . ."

On this same general subject of how the doctrine of the

Assumption promotes our knowledge and love of God, one must quote this observation by Fr. Bernard Leeming:

> The Assumption is an assertion that the love of the God-man has a quality of human tenderness in it, which is revealed in no other mystery of the faith. In the Bull there is repeated approbation of the feeling that Christ's affection for His mother would lead Him to want her with Him in heaven, not spiritually only, but in her bodily frame. Here at once is an indication that in the life of heaven human affections are not destroyed, even by the vision of God; and an indication that our happiness will be increased by the presence of those we loved on earth. . . . If one may reverently say so, the Assumption humanizes the God-man, and humanizes all the relations between God and man.[51]

Along with other commentators on *Munificentissimus Deus,* the same Fr. Leeming remarks that the solemn definition of the glorious Assumption of our Savior's revered associate has been instrumental in deepening the meaning of the doctrine of the redemption. His own inclination is to see in the Assumption "an assertion that God's plan of salvation is to save men through men, that human cooperation is basic to the whole plan."[52] Without rejecting this evaluation, we think it more noteworthy still that the Assumption magnifies the sovereign efficacy of the redemption. Of Mary's privileged preservation from all taint of original sin, Duns Scotus and others have remarked that this was redemption in a more sublime manner. Quite obviously, the same holds true for Our Lady's privileged preservation from bodily corruption and the dominion of death. So, then, not only the manner of her entering the world, immaculately conceived, but also the manner in which Mary left the world, already glorified in body by anticipation of the Last Day, exalts rather than detracts from the power and excellence of the redemption.

In another sense, too, is the sovereign efficacy of Our Lord's redemptive work magnified by the Assumption. For this Marian privilege highlights the completeness of Christ's victory over sin and death. In patristic teaching, the Mother of God was the first redeemed, the first to taste the fruits of the redemption. To quote St. Ambrose:

> The Lord, when He undertook to redeem the world, began His work with Mary, in order that she, through whom salvation was prepared for all, might be the first to enjoy the fruit of salvation from the hand of her Son.[53]

Against this background of patristic doctrine, one can now appreciate the profound remark of a fifteenth-century theologian, Gabriel Biel, that if Mary—she who above all should benefit by the fruits of the redemption—has not been assumed bodily into heaven, then Christ has not won in any instance a total triumph over sin and death. And this would look like defeat.[54] Since Pope Pius XII's solemn definition on Nov. 1, 1950, even the mere appearance of such a defeat has been banished forever. The sovereign efficacy of Christ's death on the cross stands forth before all the world. Mary, immaculately conceived, is also Mary assumed into heaven, body and soul. As such, she is the epiphany of the redemption in all its fullness. She is the shining trophy of Christ's sweeping victory over sin and death. "Mary's Assumption crowns the work of salvation, since it shows that the salvific work of Christ is now absolute and perfect in at least one person." [55]

By the same token, Our Lady's bodily Assumption into heaven confirms another article of Christian belief, the eventual participation of all the just in the full fruits of the redemption—"the resurrection of the body and life everlasting." However, this point can be more conveniently developed in the next and last portion of our paper, to which we now turn, on the significance of the doctrine of the Assumption for our times.

An all-wise providence governs God's disclosures to humanity. Public Revelation was not given to mankind all at once, but progressively, over a period of centuries, according to the divine plan. As the Epistle to the Hebrews states: "God, who in many portions and in divers manners spoke in times past to the fathers by the prophets, last of all in these days has spoken to us by his Son." [56]

Even after the termination of that progressive Revelation, with the death of the last Apostle, it still remained for the Church, again under God's providence, to take inventory of the revealed truths, to grow increasingly conscious of the endless riches of the deposit of faith.

Hence it was that some truths began to dawn on the Church only after a while. Among these one must number that of Our Lady's bodily Assumption. For, in all probability, this Marian prerogative was not explicitly professed in the faith of the first Christian centuries.[57] In due course, however, when the Church found time and occasion to concentrate on the mystery of the Blessed Mother's final lot, that great privilege asserted itself in the Christian consciousness, and constantly gained in clarity over the centuries until, in our own day, it has stood forth with utmost brilliance.[58]

That the consummation of this process of explicitation, the solemn definition of the dogma of the Assumption, was reserved for our own age is a striking dispensation of Divine Providence. For never did an age so sorely need the solace and inspiration which come to us from this great Marian truth. A century ago, Pius IX, the Pope of the Immaculate Conception, although he was utterly certain of the revealed character of the Assumption, declined the petition of Queen Isabella II of Spain, that this Marian privilege be solemnly defined as a dogma of faith. The time is not yet ripe for such a definition, the Sovereign Pontiff explained,[59] but he added that that time would surely come, under God. And come it did, on Nov. 1, 1950. As Pope Pius XII himself declared, just before proceeding to his infallible definition:

> We believe that the moment appointed in the plan of divine Providence for the solemn proclamation of this outstanding privilege of the Virgin Mary has already arrived.[60]

That the dogma did indeed have, under God, a special appointment with the mid-twentieth century, is then brought home to us by these words of the Holy Father:

> And so may we hope that those who meditate upon the glorious example Mary offers us may be more and more convinced of the value of a human life entirely devoted to carrying out the heavenly Father's will and to bringing good to others. Thus, while the

illusory teachings of materialism and the corruption of morals that follows from these teachings threaten to extinguish the light of virtue and to ruin the lives of men by exciting discord among them, in this magnificent way all may see clearly to what a lofty goal our bodies and souls are destined. Finally, it is our hope that belief in Mary's bodily Assumption into Heaven will make our belief in our own resurrection stronger and render it more effective.[61]

Here, then, is the Pope's own evaluation of the providential role of the dogma of the Assumption precisely for our times. He alerts us to the fact that the newly defined doctrine by no means bears on the Blessed Mother alone. On the contrary, it is of personal import for every member of the human race. Far from being an exclusively Mariological truth, the dogma has powerful overtones, profound implications, for Christian anthropology and eschatology. That is to say, it teaches us not only about Mary but also about ourselves, and our final lot. Hence the dogma is diametrically opposed to the paramount, the most pernicious, errors of the day—errors about man's nature, dignity, and ultimate destiny. Accordingly, a lively faith in the dogma of the Assumption, in all that it presupposes and implies, will serve as a salutary antidote to those errors and their attendant evils.

One cannot improve upon, one can only unfold and expand this, the Holy Father's explanation of why his solemn definition is so opportune for the twentieth century. Attempting such a commentary, we must begin by emphasizing that the troubles of this century derive chiefly from misconceptions about the meaning and destiny of man. "All systems of politics, of sociology and of morality," Valéry remarked, "are inspired by a single conception which man has of man." A correct concept of man is, therefore, the very cornerstone of the entire social order; errors about the "what" and the "whither" of human existence inexorably work havoc on every level of the human community.

Baneful errors of this sort there have always been. But, in the century which has elapsed since Pius IX foretold that the future would surely bring the right moment for a definition of the Assumption, false teachings on the make-up, dignity, and goal of man have achieved an unprecedented growth and spread, and they, more than any other factor, are responsible for the social, political, and international disorders which so grievously afflict the present generation. As the United States Hierarchy declared not many years ago:

> At the bottom of all problems of the world today is the problem of man. Unless those who bear the responsibility of world leadership are in basic agreement on what man is, there is no way out of the confusion and conflict which block the road to real peace.[62]

Our Bishops were but echoing what has been the constant cry of the modern Popes, from Leo XIII to Pius XII —the warning that there can be no reconstruction of our shattered social order unless there be a return to the Christian concept of man. "The Church," Pius XII affirmed in his 1944 Christmas Message, "has the mission to announce to the world, which is looking for better and more perfect forms of democracy, the highest and most needed message that there can be: the dignity of man, the call to be sons of God."

It was in the interests of this urgent mission of the Church, it was to proclaim anew and with new force this "highest and most needed message," that the Holy Father, by his solemn definition, focused world attention on Our Lady's bodily Assumption into heavenly glory. The dogma's lessons for contemporary humanity will be better appreciated in their timeliness if we preface a summary of them with a resume of the main errors of our age concerning man. One finds these errors referred to, either expressly or by allusion, in the Pope's own vindication of the opportuneness of his dogmatic definition, which was quoted above. They are, on the one hand, atheistic materialism and naturalism; on the other, an inhuman spiritualism and an exaggerated supernaturalism.

Of these errors the foremost and most pernicious is, of course, atheistic materialism (along with what is practically indistinguishable from it, naturalism). That this doctrine is the most formidable danger of our day was well emphasized by the Bishops of the United States in their statement, "Victory—Our Faith": [63]

> Our concern is aroused by a tyranny already imposed upon a billion souls. It threatens the destruction of our own land as it has already attacked the culture of others. That tyranny is atheistic materialism, whether revealed in communism or in godless humanism. . . . Whether it be entrenched in the organs of a foreign state, or in one of our own domestic institutions, it is atheistic materialism that seeks to destroy us. This is the enemy.

Acknowledging but one reality, matter, atheistic materialism assaults not only God but also His image, man.

According to its macabre teachings, the body is the whole of man, and for him there is no life other than that which ends here below; *homo sapiens* is but a brute, possessed of no spiritual character, no intrinsic dignity, no sacred rights, no immortal destiny.

An age-old error, to be sure, but one which was never so rampant as in the present century. Of the many factors which account for its cancerous growth we shall mention only one. For the first time in history, atheistic materialism has been translated into a revolutionary movement, has become a militant philosophy of government, has won the support of powerful sovereign states—the Soviet Union and its satellites. By force of arms and by ceaseless propaganda, these godless governments strive to impose their materialistic views on the entire human race.

We cannot here rehearse all the evil consequences of atheistic materialism in the practical order. That has been done in detail by the sovereign pontiffs, from Leo XIII to Pius XII. In particular, these have warned, and *Munificentissimus Deus* repeats the warning (in the passage we are unfolding), that the doctrine leads to what Bishop John J. Wright has termed "two superficially opposed extremes: a perverse cult of the body on the one hand, the cruel abuse of bodies on the other." As Pius XII observed on an earlier occasion: "Take away respect for God . . . (and) men consequently find their solace only in the pursuit of pleasure; and then, unleashing their fury, they hurl themselves like beasts on one another in mutual destruction." [64] In incontrovertible fact, atheistic materialism (aided by the tremendous technical progress of the last one hundred years) has given rise to an era of lustful self-indulgence unparalleled in history; and, incarnate in the communist states, it has been responsible for that cult of violence and that contempt for the value of human life which, in the words of Christopher Dawson, has swept like an epidemic over vast regions of the globe.

Atheistic materialism and naturalism are not alone in deforming the true image of man, with disastrous consequences for man himself. For, in addition to those perverse doctrines which acknowledge only the material, the natural and the here and now, we must note, this time within the ranks of those who call themselves Christians, certain errors which go to the opposite extreme, currents of thought which acknowledge or value only the spiritual, the supernatural, and the hereafter. The aberrations in question are: an exaggerated spiritualism, and an exaggerated supernaturalism.

In its most crass form, exaggerated spiritualism denies the reality of things material, and therefore also of the human body. We dismiss this patent absurdity and confine ourselves rather to what may be termed "angelism." This form of exaggerated spiritualism abhors or disdains the flesh, while erring at times also regarding the union between soul and body, as though the latter did not have a rightful and indispensable place in the human composite.

The most notorious manifestations of this attitude are to be found in the non-Christian, respectively, non-Catholic, doctrines of Docetism, Gnosticism, Manichaeism, Albigensianism, and Protestantism.[65] However, Catholic circles have not been altogether free from the blight of angelism. There have been and still are Catholic rigorists, inimical to the flesh, whose piety has been described as being "to all intents and purposes platonistic." [66] And one must acknowledge the vogue, at least in the not too distant past, of a theology more Cartesian than Thomist; a theology ignorant or forgetful of the truth that man is incarnate spirit, the truth that body and soul, far from being merely juxtaposed, are intimately joined in a substantial union, with the material element profoundly influencing the spiritual; a theology oblivious to the fact that the whole man was made to the image and likeness of God, whence the body is not without share in that resemblance; a theology readier to speak of the immortality of the soul than of the resurrection of the body.[67]

In fine, there have been Catholics deaf to Tertullian's profound observation, "salvation hinges on the flesh (*caro salutis est cardo*)"; Catholics also who repudiated his other classic statement, "the resurrection of the dead is the Christian's trust (*fiducia Christianorum resurrectio mortuorum*)." [68] How many of the faithful today are infected by angelism, and to what degree, it would be impossible to say. But there is reason to suspect that not a few give little more than half-hearted assent to the Creed when it professes faith in "the resurrection of the body." [69] Mauriac betrayed such faint-heartedness when he wrote, shortly before the definition of the Assumption:

> But we Christians, do we really believe in eternal life? The dogma of the Assumption, so disconcerting for many minds—and, I confess it, for myself—which the Holy Father is going to define on the Feast of All Saints, draws our attention to that article of the Creed, the most mysterious, the most incredible, which is so rarely discussed by the Church and which represents an insane, a marvellous hope—the resurrection of the flesh . . .[70]

As to the faithful who do wholeheartedly profess that "most incredible" article of the Creed, more often than not they look upon the resurrection of the body only as something quite incidental, rather than as an integral part of their destiny and the consummation of the work of our redemption.[71] Lost upon most is the full meaning of Christ's exhortation regarding His second coming, when He will raise us up in the flesh: "But when these things begin to come to pass, look up, and lift up your heads, because your redemption is at hand!" [72]

Angelism's disdain for things material is shared by exaggerated supernaturalism. But the latter error goes much further, extending its disdain to all terrestrial realities. In a misguided attempt to do full justice to the order of grace and salvation 'ultrasupernaturalism' values only transcendent realities, the supra-temporal, extra-spatial, and celestial. It negates the worth of this world, of life here below, of human effort and temporal activity; whence ultrasupernaturalism is also known as "quietism."

It is neither possible nor necessary to distinguish here the manifold forms and degrees in which this error has taken hold of Christians in times past. Monsignor Ronald A. Knox has done all that for us in his *Enthusiasm,* which is, in effect, a history of ultrasupernaturalism.[73] Suffice it to remark that some modern Catholics have been among the exponents of that pseudo-Christian attitude toward the "here and now." Pope Pius XII reprehended them not only in well-known passages of the Encyclicals *Mystici Corporis Christi* and *Mediator Dei,*[74] but also on an earlier occasion, in a discourse commemorating the fiftieth anniversary of *Rerum novarum.* In that pronouncement the Holy Father, after reminding the laity of their moral obligation to cooperate in the regeneration of society, and especially of economic life, went on to warn:

102

Do not let yourselves be misled by the manufacturers of error and unhealthy theories, those deplorable trends not of increase but of decomposition and of corruption of the religious life: currents of thought which hold that since redemption belongs to the sphere of supernatural grace, and is therefore exclusively the work of God, there is no need for us to cooperate on earth. . . . As if the first efficacy of grace were not to cooperate with our sincere efforts to fulfill every day the commandments of God, as individuals and members of society; as if for the last two thousand years there had not lived nor persevered in the soul of the Church the sense of the collective responsibility of all for all. . . .[75]

A decade later, two short years after his definition of the Assumption, the Sovereign Pontiff renewed the above warning in these words:

A supernaturalism that holds itself aloof, and especially one that keeps religion aloof, from economic and political needs and duties, as if these did not concern the Christian and the Catholic, is something unhealthy, alien to the thinking of the Church.[76]

Justly does Pius XII label ultrasupernaturalism as an "unhealthy theory," a "deplorable trend." Among other evil effects, it stifles human initiative, paralyzes Catholic Action, and precludes in advance any theology of social progress.[77] Above all, together with inhuman spiritualism or angelism, it has contributed, indirectly but considerably, to the spread of materialism, in that it leaves Christianity open to the reproach of being a doctrine foreign to man and his problems, indifferent to his present miseries.[78]

Such, then, are the leading and most fateful errors of our times; all have contributed to the contemporary crisis of humanity. To counteract and correct them has been a chief preoccupation of the modern Popes. Given this background, we can now fully appreciate the providential character of the solemn definition of the Blessed Mother's Assumption, body and soul, into heavenly glory. That definition commanded world-wide attention for what is, in effect, an incomparable epitome of papal teaching on the Christian concept of man and man's authentic goal.

It is no accident that the dogma was proclaimed on the Feast of All Saints, rather than on August 15th or any other feast of Our Lady. That date was chosen to awaken us to the fact that what the dogma tells us about the Blessed Virgin is not the whole of its message. In addition to its specifically Marian content, the dogma teaches us about man generally. It projects and silhouettes man in his true dimensions, against his true horizon. The solemn definition of Our Lady's glorious Assumption stands forth as a timely—indeed, desperately needed—affirmation of Christian Humanism. Over against atheistic materialism and naturalism on the one hand, and exaggerated spiritualism and ultrasupernaturalism on the other hand, Christian Humanism declares man for what he really is, a creature composed of body and soul, and made to the image and likeness of God; Christian Humanism upholds the value and dignity of human beings in body and soul; Christian Humanism acknowledges the worth of life here on earth but, at the same time, warns that our destiny is not confined to this world; and, finally, as to that destiny—supernatural salvation, Christian Humanism insists that it is not purely spiritual but embraces the whole man, body as well as soul—in short, the human person.[79]

Let us spell out some of these precious lessons of our dogma; first, as to the make-up of man. Mary is, after all, of exactly the same nature as ourselves. Hence the defined truth that, having completed the course of her earthly life, she was assumed body and soul into heavenly glory attests, against materialism and exaggerated spiritualism, that man is neither body only nor soul only, but a composite of both. Nor are these elements merely juxtaposed, as angelism tends to hold. The glorification of Our Lady's body confirms the corporeal-spiritual unity of the human person, the substantial union of soul and body; for it is only by reason of such a union that the glorified soul can effect the glorious transformation of the risen flesh.[80]

Further, Our Lady's Assumption hammers home the truth about man's real last end; the truth that, though we live in time and space, we are headed toward a goal which lies beyond both; the truth that, though part of the created universe, we are destined to share, body and soul, in the glory and joy of the Creator. For Mary's final lot was a privileged one only in that her body was spared the corruption of the tomb and did not have to wait until the end of time for its entry into heavenly glory. The dogma of the Assumption exhibits the Blessed Mother as the first-fruits of the redemption, not the entire harvest. If her total glorification was privileged only in that it was "anticipated," this implies that total glorification is ultimately in store for others. Mary's consummated victory over death is a dramatic preview of our own, a gage and reminder of the glorious reunion awaiting the souls and bodies of all the just.

Granted, such a gage and reminder mankind already had in the Resurrection and Ascension of Christ. But, as Gabriel Biel suggested, even more than Christ's conquest of death can that vouchsafed to Mary conciliate and deepen faith in the Creed's "resurrection of the body and life everlasting." Because Christ is no mere creature but the God-man, Christians tinged with angelism, from Paul's Corinthians (cf. 1 Corinthians 15) down to Mauriac, have mistakenly hesitated to see in Our Lord's resurrection a gage of their own. Mary, however, is purely human. Hence the dogma of her Assumption should banish all diffidence about the resurrection of mere men; it is logical and psychologically effective proof that even this mortal frame of ours can be made to triumph over death. With reason, therefore, Pius XII expressed the "hope that belief in Mary's bodily Assumption into heaven will make our belief in our own resurrection stronger and render it more effective."

It was the Sovereign Pontiff's further hope "that those who meditate upon the glorious example Mary offers us may be more and more convinced of the value of a human life entirely devoted to carrying out the heavenly Father's will and to bringing good to others." From these papal words we gather that the dogma of the Assumption, while teaching us to lift our gaze and direct our hopes beyond the frontiers of earth, discourages rather than supports ultrasupernaturalism. Pius XII reminds us that our glorious resurrection and future happiness must be merited, by a life penetrated with charity. Thus the doctrine of the Assumption acknowledges the worth and necessity of the here and the now, of temporal activity, of human effort cooperating with grace; it is "a pressing invitation to a life of sincere and practical love towards God and neighbor, a love which constitutes the synthesis of the whole Law." [81]

That "the glorious example" of Mary demonstrates, against ultrasupernaturalism, "the value of a human life entirely devoted to carrying out the heavenly Father's will and to bringing good to others" comes home to us especially when we reflect that the Blessed Mother's "anticipated" full redemption was a postponed one. That is to say, Mary was already deserving of her full eternal reward when her divine Son ascended into heaven—worthier by far than those "saints" of Matthew 27:52–53, who in all probability were taken up body and soul in company with Christ. "But, though worthy of heaven, she abides a while on earth, so that the infant Church may be directed and comforted by her. . . ." [82] Constituted the Spiritual Mother of mankind, "with a generous heart Mary undertook and discharged the duties of her high but laborious office, the beginnings of which were consecrated in the Cenacle. With wonderful care she nutured the first Christians by her holy example, her authoritative counsel, her sweet consolation, her fruitful prayers. . . ." [83]

Truly, then, the dogma of the Assumption is a compendium of Christian Humanism, reconciling the spiritual with the material, things heavenly with things earthly, the life of time with the life of eternity. It exhibits man in his total reality, composed at the same time of body and soul, an individual person and member of society, a citizen of this earth and one chosen for heaven. As a deterrent to totalitarianism, it proclaims the true dignity of the human being—incarnate spirit, person, image of God, and therefore subject of certain inviolable rights which no State may set aside. As a deterrent to lustful indulgence of one's own flesh and to violence toward that of others, it underscores the sacredness of the human body—a body raised to the honor of being the dwelling-place and instrument of the Spirit, meant moreover to be on earth God's special temple, and destined eventually to rejoin the soul in His beatific presence. As a deterrent to pessimism and despair, it reassures the world's unfortunates and oppressed that "God will wipe away every tear from their eyes, and death shall be no more; neither shall there be mourning, nor crying nor pain any more" (Apocalypse 21:4). As a deterrent to practical materialism, it admonishes those who rejoice in this world's goods not to forget that "eye has not seen nor ear heard, nor has it entered into the heart of man, what things God has prepared for those who love Him" (1 Corinthians 2:9).

Such, in the main, are the salutary lessons of Our Lady's Assumption for modern man. Clearly, it was the will of Providence that the dogma be defined at this stage of history, and that the happy event should coincide with the end of the Holy Year appointed by Pius XII to effect "the Great Return of mankind to the Divine Plan." [84]

NOTES

[1] Cf. W. Doheny, J. Kelly (editors), *Papal Documents on Mary* (Milwaukee, 1954), pp. 25 (*Ineffabilis Deus*), 238, 239 (*Munificentissimus Deus*).

[2] *Ibid.*, pp. 9–10.

[3] *Ibid.*, p. 11.

[4] *Ibid.*, p. 237.

[5] For the obligatory character of such teachings, cf. the Encyclical "Humani generis" (Aug. 12, 1950), in A. Cotter, *The Encyclical 'Humani generis,'* second edition, (Weston, 1952), pp. 21 f.; for a commentary on the passage, cf. *ibid.*, pp. 79–82.

[6] Doheny-Kelly, *op. cit.*, pp. 237–238.

[7] *Ibid.*, p. 239.

[8] Cf. *Munificentissimus Deus;* in Doheny-Kelly, *op. cit.*, pp. 222–223, 224–225, 238, 239.

[9] Cf. *ibid.*, pp. 221–222.

[10] *Ibid.*, p. 222.

[11] Quoted in *Munificentissimus Deus* (Doheny-Kelly, *op. cit.*, p. 234).

[12] "Allocutio cum legeretur decretum de tuto pro canonizatione Beatae Thouret," in *Osservatore Romano*, Aug. 16–17, 1933.

[13] B. Mascall, "Gedanken eines Anglokatholiken ueber die Definition der Himmelfahrt Marias," in *Oekumenische Einheit*, II, 2 (1951), 140.

[14] Cf. *Catechism of the Council of Trent*, I, chapter 7.

[15] Cf. *The New York Times*, Nov. 11, 1950.

[16] Cf. I. Filograssi, "Constitutio Apostolica 'Munificentissimus Deus' de Assumptione Beatae Mariae Virginis," in *Gregorianum*, XXXI (1950), p. 520, note 54.

17 Cf. F. Diekamp, *Theologiae Dogmaticae Manuale,* Vol. IV (Parisiis: Desclee et Sociorum; n.d.) p. 497; *Catechism of the Council of Trent,* IV, chapter 9.

18 The Latin original of "unique triumph" in Doheny-Kelly, *op. cit.,* p. 226, is "singularem . . . triumphum."

19 *Ibid.,* p. 222: "an entirely unique triumph."

20 *Loc. cit.*

21 Cf. F. Prat, *Jesus Christ* (translated by J. Heenan), Vol. II (Milwaukee, n.d.; copyright 1950), p. 399.

22 Cf. H. Zeller, "Corpora Sanctorum: Eine Studie zu Mt 27, 52–53," in *Zeitschrift fuer katholische Theologie,* LXXI (1949), 385–465; K. Rahner, *Das 'Neue' Dogma: Zur Definition der Himmelfahrt der hl. Jungfrau und Gottesmutter* (Wien, 1951; reprinted from *Wort und Wahrheit,* Nov., 1950), p. 35.

23 Cf. Rahner, *op. cit.,* pp. 8–11.

24 Cf. W. McGarry, "A Fundamental Principle in Mariology," in *Theological Studies,* I (1940), 396–411; II (1941), 35–52. The principle applies, of course, to privileges which are not incompatible with Mary's condition, role, and dignity.

25 Cf. Rahner, *op. cit.,* pp. 34–35.

26 Cf. Doheny-Kelly, *op. cit.,* p. 225.

27 Cf. G. Roschini, *La Madonna secondo la Fede e la Teologia,* Vol. III (Roma, 1953), pp. 231–232; Filograssi, *art. cit.,* pp. 490, 524 with note 62; A. Kolping, "Zur theologischen Erkenntnismethode anlaesslich der Definition der leiblichen Aufnahme Mariens in den Himmel," in *Divus Thomas* (Fribourg), XXIX (1951), 103–105.

28 Cf. Kolping, *art. cit.,* pp. 103–105.

29 *Munificentissimus Deus,* in Doheny-Kelly, *op. cit.,* p. 224.

30 Cf. B. Leeming, "The Assumption and the Christian Pattern," in *The Month,* CXCI (March, 1951), 146.

31 Doheny-Kelly, *op. cit.,* pp. 221, 225, 226–227, 230, 237, 238.

32 Suarez, *De Religione,* tract. II, 1. II, c. VIII, n. 8; in *Opera omnia,* ed. Vives, t. XIII, p. 283. Cf. J. Duhr, S.J., *The Glorious Assumption of the Mother of God* (New York, n.d.; copyright, 1950), p. 54.

33 *Munificentissimus Deus,* in Doheny-Kelly, *op. cit.,* p. 237.

34 Encyclical *Supremi Apostolatus* (Sept. 1, 1883); in Doheny-Kelly, *op. cit.,* p. 29.

[35] Pius XI, Epist. *Auspicatus profecto* (Jan. 28, 1933); in *Acta Apostolicae Sedis,* XXV (1933), p. 80. Cf. Pius XII, Encycl. *Ad Caeli Reginam* (Oct. 11, 1954); English translation in Marian Reprint No. 30 (The Marian Library, University of Dayton, Dayton, Ohio), p. 7, and in *The Catholic Mind,* LIII (Jan., 1955), 55.

[36] *The Book of Genesis, translated . . . by members of the Catholic Biblical Association of America* (Paterson, 1948).

[37] Cf. D. Unger, O.F.M. Cap., *The First-Gospel: Genesis 3, 15* (St. Bonaventure, N.Y., 1954); E. May, O.F.M. Cap., "Mary in the Old Testament," in J. Carol, O.F.M. (editor), *Mariology,* Vol. I (Milwaukee, 1955), pp. 56–62.

[38] Cf. D. Nerney, "The Assumption of Our Lady," in *The Irish Ecclesiastical Record,* LXXXII (Aug., 1954), 74–79.

[39] Cf. *Ineffabilis Deus,* in Doheny-Kelly, *op. cit.,* pp. 17–18.

[40] *Ad Caeli Reginam* (Oct. 11, 1954); Marian Reprint No. 30 (The Marian Library, University of Dayton, Dayton, Ohio), p. 7; *The Catholic Mind,* LIII (Jan., 1955), 55.

[41] Cf. Doheny-Kelly, *op. cit.,* p. 237; for a commentary on this argument, cf. J. Carol, O.F.M., "The Apostolic Constitution 'Munificentissimus Deus' and Our Blessed Lady's Coredemption," in *The American Ecclesiastical Review,* CXXV (Oct., 1951), 255–273.

[42] Cf. Doheny-Kelly, *op. cit.,* pp. 236, 238.

[43] *Ibid.,* pp. 221–222.

[44] Cf. Pius XII, Encycl. *Fulgens Corona* (Sept. 8, 1953); Doheny-Kelly, *op. cit.,* p. 259.

[45] Cf. Pius XII, Encycl. *Ad Caeli Reginam* (Oct. 11, 1954).

[46] For the arguments and a discussion of their value, cf. various articles in the Assumption issue of *The Thomist,* XIV (Jan., 1951), by C. Friethoff, G. Roschini, and K. Healy; cf. also J. Carol, "The Definability of Mary's Assumption," in *The American Ecclesiastical Review,* CXVIII (March, 1948), 161–177.

[47] Cf. *Munificentissimus Deus,* in Doheny-Kelly, *op. cit.,* pp. 223–225, 237–238.

[48] Cf. Filograssi, *art. cit.,* in *Gregorianum,* XXXI (1950), 522; M. Gordillo, "La Bula de la Asuncion," in *Estudios Eclesiasticos,* XXV (Jul.–Sept., 1951), 340–341; L. Colomer, "Incitamentos Marianos en la Bula 'Munificentissimus Deus'," in *Estudios Marianos,* XII (1952), 169–189.

[49] Cf. L. Brou, "Marie, destructrice de toutes les hérésies," in

Ephemerides Liturgicae, LXI (1948), 321–353; J. de Tonquedec, "Cunctas haereses sola interemisti . . . ," in *Nouvelle Revue Théologique,* LXXXVI (Sept.–Oct., 1954), 858–862; J. Fenton, "Our Lady and the Extirpation of Heresy," in Fenton-Benard (editors), *Studies in Praise of Our Blessed Mother* (Washington, D.C., 1952), pp. 231–243.

50 Cf. Chapter I.

51 *Art. cit.,* in *The Month,* CXCI (March, 1951), 149–150.

52 *Ibid.,* 148–149, 150.

53 Cf. St. Ambrose, *Expositio Evangelii secundum Lucam,* lib. II, n. 17; Migne, *Patrologia Latina,* Vol. 15, col. 1559.

54 Cf. J. Duhr, *op. cit.,* p. 66.

55 C. Friethoff, O.P., "The Dogmatic Definition of the Assumption," in *The Thomist,* XIV (Jan., 1951), p. 58. In this connection we cannot refrain from quoting the rather remarkable testimony of a Russian Orthodox theologian, Vl. Lossky, *Essai sur la Théologie mystique de l'Orient* (Paris, 1944), p. 190: "To say that no human person has yet attained to perfect union with God would be to misunderstand the very heart of the Church, one of her most secret mysteries, her mystic center, her perfection already realized in one human person fully united with God, a person whose resurrection and judgment have already been accomplished. This person is Mary, the Mother of God. . . . But death had no further hold on her: like her Son, she was raised to life and taken up into heaven,—the first human person who realizes in herself the last end for which the world was created. In consequence, the Church and the whole universe have from now on their completion, their personal summit which opens the way for the deification of every creature." Quoted by Philips, "Problèmes de la Théologie Mariale," in *Marianum,* XI (1949), 52, who asks: "Will anyone still maintain that the Assumption is an accessory detail?"

56 Hebrews 1, 1; "in many portions" (rather than "at sundry times") is the correct rendering of the Greek text.

57 Cf. H. Zeller, "Corpora Sanctorum: Eine Studie zu Mt 27, 52–53," in *Zeitschrift fuer katholische Theologie,* XXXI (1949), 464. That the truth of the Assumption was not yet to the fore in the first Christian centuries can be construed as another dispensation of Providence; cf. F. Dander, S.J., *Mariologia,* in L. Lercher, S.J., *Institutiones Theologiae Dogmaticae,* Vol. III, ed.

3 (Oeniponte-Lipsiae, 1942), n. 318, obj. 2; M. J. Scheeben, *Handbuch der Katholischen Dogmatik*, Vol. V/2, ed. 2, edited by C. Feckes (Freiburg im Br., 1954), n. 1738, with footnote 6.

[58] Cf. *Munificentissimus Deus,* in Doheny-Kelly, *op. cit.,* p. 221.

[59] Letter of Queen Isabella II, Feb. 3, 1864; quoted in G. Hentrich, S.J., R. De Moos, S.J., *Petitiones de Assumptione Corporea B. V. Mariae in caelum definienda ad Sanctam Sedem deletae,* Vol. II (Typis Polyglottis Vaticanis, 1942), p. 576.

[60] *Munificentissimus Deus,* in Doheny-Kelly, *op. cit.,* p. 238.

[61] *Ibid.,* pp. 238–239.

[62] Statement on "Man and the Peace," Nov. 17, 1946; cf. R. Huber, O.F.M.Conv. (editor), *Our Bishops Speak* (Milwaukee, 1952), p. 131.

[63] Nov. 21, 1954; cf. *The Catholic Mind,* LIII (Feb., 1955), 125.

[64] "Exhortation on Atheism," Feb. 11, 1949; cf. *Catholic Documents,* No. II (The Pontifical Court Club, London, 1950), p. 6.

[65] Cf. P. Palmer, S.J., "Mary and the Flesh," in T. Burke, S.J. (ed.), *Mary and Modern Man* (New York, 1954), pp. 111–134.

[66] Cf. *ibid.,* pp. 134–140; G. Sinaldi, O.P., "Assumption: présentation de l'humanité parfaite," in *Marie* (Nicolet, Canada), March–April, 1951, pp. 139–141; S. Moore, O.S.B., in *The Downside Review,* Jan. 1955, p. 95, reviewing G. Siewerth, *Der Mensch und sein Leib* (Einsiedeln: Johannes Verlag).

[67] Cf. S. Moore, *ubi supra;* R. Aubert, *La théologie catholique au milieu du XXᵉ siècle* (Tournai-Paris, 1954), p. 62; J. Newman, "The Theology of Social Action," in *The Irish Theological Quarterly,* XXII (Jan., 1955), 31. According to St. Thomas Aquinas (*De potentia,* 5, 10, ad 2), the soul in its attachment to the body bears a greater resemblance to God than when separated from the body; Cf. M. Schmaus, *Katholische Dogmatik,* Vol. II (Muenchen, 1949), pp. 294–295; cf. *ibid.,* pp. 287–292.

[68] Cf. Tertullian, *De carnis resurrectione,* 5; *ibid.,* 2.

[69] Cf. K. Rahner, S.J., "Auferstehung des Fleisches," in *Stimmen der Zeit,* LXXIX (Nov., 1953), 81–91; Dr. Grosche, "Zum Dogma der Himmelfahrt Mariä," in *Herder-Korrespondenz,* V (Jan.–Feb., 1951), 210–211.

[70] Cf. *The (London) Tablet,* Nov. 4, 1950, 384, quoting and commenting on Mauriac's statement.

[71] K. Rahner, S.J., *Das 'Neue' Dogma* (Wien, 1951), *passim.*

[72] Matthew 21, 28.

[73] R. Knox *Enthusiasm* (New York and Oxford, 1950); cf. pp. 2, 3, 350.

[74] Cf. Pius XII, Encycl. Letter *The Mystical Body of Christ* (June 29, 1943); New York: The America Press, nn. 101–102; Encycl. Letter *On the Sacred Liturgy* (Nov. 20, 1947); N.C.W.C. ed. (Vatican Library translation), n. 203.

[75] Pius XII, Discourse on the Feast of Pentecost, June 1, 1941; *AAS*, XXXIII (June 23, 1941), pp. 225–226.

[76] Pius XII, Address to members of *Pax Christi* (Sept. 20, 1952); in *The Catholic Mind*, Sept., 1953, 565. Cf. also the Holy Father's address to the International Convention of Humanistic Studies, Sept. 25, 1949, in *The Catholic Mind*, May, 1950, 317. See, in addition, the late Cardinal Suhard's protests against Quietism; e.g., in his "Growth or Decline?", in *The Church Today* (Chicago, 1953), pp. 136, 138. Note current criticisms of an unbalanced "Theology of Transcendence," in Aubert, *op. cit.*, pp. 60–70.

[77] Cf. J. Newman, "The Theology of Social Action," in *The Irish Theological Quarterly*, XXII (Jan., 1955), 31–48.

[78] *Ibid.*, 40–41; Aubert, *op. cit.*, p. 63; G. Thils, *Théologie des réalités terrestres*, Vol. I, ed. 2 (Bruges-Paris, 1946), pp. 35–36.

[79] On Christian Humanism, see H. Sacher, "Humanismus," in H. Sacher-O. v. Nell-Breuning (edd.), *Woerterbuch der Politik*, Heft V (*Gesellschaftliche Ordnungsysteme*), erste Lieferung (Freib. im Br., 1951), col. 116–120.

[80] Cf. St. Thomas Aquinas, *De Veritate*, XXVI, 10 ad 2, 16.

[81] G. Roschini, O.S.M., *Il Dogma dell' Assunzione*, ed. 2 (Roma, 1951), p. 142.

[82] Pope Leo XIII, Encycl. *Iucunda semper* (Sept. 8, 1894); in Doheny-Kelly, *op. cit.*, p. 93.

[83] Pope Leo XIII, Encycl. *Adiutricem populi* (Sept. 5, 1895); in Doheny-Kelly, *op. cit.*, p. 102; cf. Pius XII, Encycl. Letter *The Mystical Body of Christ*, The America Press ed., no. 130.

[84] Cf. the Holy Father's Homily on the Assumption, Oct. 30, 1950, in *The Catholic Mind*, Jan., 1951, 79; and compare with the lessons of the Assumption the Sovereign Pontiff's 1949 Christmas Message on the Holy Year (text in V. Yzermans, ed., *The Unwearied Advocate*, Vol. III, pp. 58–67).

114

Our Lady in Our Land

DANIEL SARGENT

Our Lady in Our Land

Who was it first uttered a prayer to Our Lady in our land? We shall never know, but we do know his prayer. It was the prayer of a man who is lost, and who knows he is lost, the prayer of a man who is shipwrecked, and is alive yet knows he cannot return home. It was the cry of distress, the commonest prayer of all Christians to Our Lady, the plea for mercy: "Pray for us now and at the hour of our death."

From that first prayer till now a thousand years have passed—a half of the time that has elapsed since the birth of Our Lord—and during those thousand years millions on millions of prayers have been raised in our land to Our Lady that bore Our Lord. They have all echoed that first prayer, but to that echo they have added various praises of her, according to the circumstances of those who prayed, and also according to the devotions which they had been taught. There is a story to those prayers which has affected and reflected the story of our land.

From the year 1000 to 1400 there were from time to time Christians treading on our shores who had been more than merely shipwrecked on them, and who returned to their lands, and had a certain renown for having trodden them. They were Norse and only Norse. They came to our land not to explore, and yet not by mistake. The Norse had settled in Greenland, and they needed timber which did not grow in Greenland, and they were seeking it in regions to the southwest in our land. They must have recited prayers to Our Lady, for they were Christians and had a bishopric in Greenland. But what was the nature of their prayers to her?

The first of these Norsemen who is known, was Leif Ericson, who came in 1002 to a land which he called Vinland because there were grapes growing on it, and which has been identified as New England. He was a Christian and an ardent apostolic one, and a convert. When he came to a land which he found so delectable as to compliment it by likening it to the vine-growing shores of the Mediterranean, to which his kin were flocking, he must have done more than pray to Our Lady for mercy. He surely gave thanks to her, but how? With an *Ave Maria?* No, for that salutation was not current anywhere in Europe at the time. It is likely that he hailed her as *Star of the Sea,* for he had crossed a sea, black, where he needed stars, and the hymn *Ave Maris Stella* was by then two centuries old, and, without a doubt, he had heard the monks singing it in their monasteries round about the British Isles.

But what of the later Norsemen? What were their prayers? Some of them may have spent years on our shores, and, if we are to believe the Kensington Stone, they even penetrated into our land as far as Minnesota. In our forests were they still reciting the *Ave Maris Stella?*

Perhaps they were, but it is certain that by the year 1300 their more usual prayer had become the *Ave Maria.* It had spread over all of Western Europe. Again, if we believe in the Kensington Stone, it is certain that even in Minnesota an *Ave Maria* was said, for on that stone is carved, in Latin letters, A.V.M. which seems to mean *Ave Maria,* and after that, in Norse runes, the phrase "deliver us from evil." But even if we do not believe in the Stone, yet it is almost certain that by the year 1362 (which is the year carved on this Stone) Norsemen elsewhere had brought *Ave Marias* into our forests.

We can say, then, that the Norse brought the *Ave Maria* to our land but it is certain also that after 1400 they ceased to bring it. They had abandoned Greenland and needed to make no more westward voyages for timber. They had never called our land a "new world." They had looked on it as an extension of the old world, a little farther on than the promontory of Norway. They had never realized how portentous it was to bring *Ave Marias* to our land. Nor would they have considered that the silence that then settled over our land was ominous—not a prayer to Our Lady left in it.—It was ominous. It was so complete that it seemed as if the bringing of *Ave Marias* had made no difference in our land's destiny, and never would.

And then in 1513 the Spaniards arrived at our land. They were led by Ponce de Leon, and the shore that they touched on was not New England, but Florida. But, without having heard of the Norseman they brought back the *Ave Marias* of the Norse to our land. And they also brought with them other prayers to Our Lady, which I call Spanish not because they had originated in Spain, but because the

Spaniards at this time had particularly appropriated them as suited to their optimistic mood. They had just, after eight hundred years of conflict, driven the Moors out of their homeland. They had sailed through the barriers of the western ocean to wondrous islands which they called the New World. Nothing seemed impossible to them. It was not that they trusted in their own powers; it was rather that they believed that Almighty God had chosen to do great things through them, and was choosing to do more. They were being entrusted to bring the Holy Faith to the uttermost parts of the earth. God had done mighty things through Our Lady because she was most pure. He was choosing to do mighty things through them, not because they were pure, but again, because she had been pure. It was because of her that all this had happened and was happening. Therefore, they were thanking her, and hailing her as *La Purisima*.

Ponce de Leon explored the Florida coast, and landed here and there on it, but he never penetrated into our land. Yet, because he had disclosed this Florida, other Spaniards did penetrate it. And where did they not go? Within fifty years they had set foot in Virginia, in the Carolinas, in Georgia, in Tennessee, in Alabama, Mississippi, Texas, Arkansas, Arizona, New Mexico, Oklahoma, Kansas, Nebraska and Colorado. They had charted our east coast from Key West to the Bay of Fundy, and our west coast from California to Oregon. They had edged about in Chesapeake Bay and called it the Bay of the Mother of God. They had built a fleet on the Mississippi. They had stared at our immense secret, the Grand Canyon. And everywhere they had gone, they had carried their prayers to La Purisima, and without these prayers they would never have gone where they did go.

There is no one who is not astounded by their exploits, but there are those who think that their prayers were a mere formality, and that their hardihood was a mere military spirit, and that their incentive was greed. There was greed, and the doughtiest of them, De Soto, had greed, but let it be remembered of him that before he began his prodigious march from Florida to Arkansas, he wrote his testament in which he ordered that, if he died in the foray, his body be brought back to Spain and there buried in a Chapel of *La Concepcion* to be erected with his own money. Let me repeat it, the Spaniards would never have gone where they did without their devotion to La Purisima.

And not only did the Spaniards sail along our coasts and march through our forests reciting their prayers to Our Lady, but they planted them on our soil. They did so by establishing in various parts of our land colonies of which the Spanish colonists prolonged those prayers, and also by teaching the prayers to the Indians. There were but two colonies of any importance that persisted, that of Saint Augustine in Florida, which was founded on Our Lady's Birthday in 1565; and that of Sante Fe, in New Mexico founded thirty-three years later. And the number of Indians who had learned to pray to Our Lady did not at any one time exceed one hundred thousand. Yet the planting is not to be mocked at. Around Saint Augustine, under the guidance of the Franciscans, there came into being a Christian Indian commonwealth which extended beyond our Florida into Georgia and the Carolinas. And about Santa Fe, the Indian Pueblos became Christian

Pueblos. And there was scarce a tribe in the space between Santa Fe and Florida that had not been visited by a missionary, and that did not know something of the God of the Christians and of the Virgin Mother. The Spaniards in our land failed to establish, except in very limited areas, the authority of the King of Spain, but they did throughout the southern half of our land spread the influence of La Purisima.

After the Spaniards had been performing their exploits for a hundred years in the southern part of our land, the French began to enter it from the northeast by way of the Saint Lawrence River. Not only did they come by a path different from that which the Spaniards had taken, but they came in a different mood from the Spanish. Politically they were not friends. Yet they resembled the first Spaniards who came to our country in this: they arrived just as a Marian century was dawning in the country from which they came. They brought with them French devotions to Our Lady as the Spaniards had brought Spanish ones.

These French devotions were not a French invention. It can be said that they were derived from Spain, as the Spanish devotions had been derived from France. Yet they had a character of their own, due to the predicament of France in the seventeenth century and to the teaching of her theologians in that period. These latter, of whom the most conspicuous were Bérulle, Olier, and Saint John Eudes, all gave great importance to Our Lady, but although they took it for granted that she had been immaculately conceived, yet they did not acclaim her as La Purisima as conspicuously as the Spaniards. They emphasized her rather as the one who gave to all Christians their supernatural life as she had given Christ His natural life. Thus the French entered our land with a particular regard for Our Lady as Mother of Christians.

Of the French who first entered our land there were a number who were more interested in making money through trading in beaver-skins than in acquiring grace from heaven, yet there was scarcely a one of them that was not a Catholic and that in moments of trial did not pray to Our Lady. But the majority of the French did far more than that. They were the French with a definite missionary spirit, priests or laymen who had come to this land only to convert the natives. They were the Frenchmen who in our land showed the greatest spirit of enterprise and leadership. These French looked on Our Lady as their leader. What were they but helpers to her in her engendering of Christians among the savages? They went everywhere they did because they felt that in so doing they were serving Our Lady, Mother of Christians.

And where did these French, accompanied by these prayers and animated by them, not go? Within seventy years of the founding of Quebec, they had explored the northern half of our land, as the Spanish had explored the southern half of it. They knew the length and breadth of the forests of Maine. They had followed the Indian paths through New York State. They had charted the southern shores of the Great Lakes, and set foot where there would be Detroit and Chicago and South Bend. They had looked at the rapids which connect Lake Superior with Lake Michigan. They had seen and heard Niagara Falls. They had become familiar with the water-ways of Wisconsin. The

Jesuit Marquette had glided down the Mississippi, which he called the River of the Immaculate Conception, to the mouth of the Arkansas.

And these French did not, any more than the Spaniards merely pass by with their prayers. They planted them. Since they had not established—not in these early years —any colonies of Frenchmen in our land, they had no French among whom they could give them root. They could only plant them among the savages upon whom they came, and as the savages were always roving in a perpetual warfare, one tribe with another, this planting was not easy. Yet a planting did take place. The prayers to Our Lady so took root in the heart of one Indian girl in New York State, a Mohawk, Catherine Tekakwitha, that she became a very beautiful and heroic child of the Mother of Christians, and has even been proposed for canonization. And they took no mean root in the hearts of the hundreds of Indians along the Great Lakes and in the Mississippi Valley who became baptized. But the planting did not end there. There were thousands and tens of thousands of Indians, who heard enough of these prayers to become preoccupied by them. The northern half of our land did not by this planting become a garden of prayers to Our Lady, but it became a region the whole aspect and manner of life of which had been changed by that planting.

Now it happened that at about the time that the French began to penetrate our land from the north, the English began to settle its east coast. These English colonists were not only preponderantly Protestants but were Protestants of Protestants. They were such fanatic Protestants as the English merchants thought would be absolutely sure to defend the English bases in the New World against the

Catholic Spanish. Such Protestants brought with them to our land not the slightest devotion to Our Lady. But amid them there happened to be a small group of English Catholics who by the whim of the English King, Charles I, had been allowed to settle and have their civil rights in the exceptional colony of Maryland. These few did bring devotions to Our Lady to our land—English ones.

In what sense were they English? The English Catholics who came to Maryland in 1634, and who celebrated their first Mass in their new home on the feast of the Annunciation, were not representative of an English Marian century. England was officially Protestant, and, if there were still a large number of Catholics in England, they were a crushed and mute people. The Catholics of England who had been allowed to take ship to the New World counted themselves lucky, for they were escaping persecution. When they arrived in Maryland they counted themselves as even more lucky. Their governor was a Catholic, and they were allowed to have Catholic priests, Jesuits, in their midst. Yet they were not without anxiety for the future. They were not thinking, like the Spanish and French, of bringing their faith to the uttermost parts of the earth. They were hoping to be able to survive and to not be molested. Their English devotion was what went with this attitude. It did not look so much to *La Purisima* and to the *Mother of Christians,* as to Our Lady who was *Queen in Heaven.* They hoped some day to be in heaven to see her but they knew that they were not there now. At times she seemed all too far away, yet she was, they were thankful to know, where she could never be dethroned, and where she could hear their prayers.

Of these English Catholics we cannot ask: "Where did

they not go?" Even the Protestant English could not go very far in our land. The Spanish were to the south and west of them, and the French to the north and west of them. They were confined to a narrow shelf of coast, and when they went faring, it was generally over the sea. But the Catholics could not go as far as the Protestants. They had to stay in Maryland. They were unwelcome in the English colonies that were Protestant. Their exploit was not in moving about, but in standing firm, in keeping their faith where they were.

And they did it well, and it was not easy. The Protestants of their own province soon turned against them, and took away their standing as equal citizens. The Catholic Marylanders were forbidden to have Catholic schools. They could not enter the liberal professions. They were doubly taxed. Yet they prayed to the Queen of Heaven, and did not lose heart, and they even showed such dignity and patience that they won the respect of the better Protestants about them. The English devotions took root. It was only in a small space, yet they went deep.

Thus, owing to the exploits of the Spanish, the French, and of Maryland Catholics, devotions to Our Lady were by the year 1700 widespread in our land. And someone from a proper vantage, surveying the general prospect of Christendom at this date, would have been justified in making the forecast that in another century all of the territory that we call our land would be filled with devotions to Our Lady. The Spaniards had made the beautiful beginning of a Christian Indian commonwealth in Florida, Georgia and the Carolinas, and this commonwealth would surely be matched by similar commonwealths from Florida to the Pacific. The French were doing something similar in the area of the Mississippi Valley, and in New York State and the province of Maine. Furthermore, there was every indication that the French, who had succeeded the Spanish as the greatest military power in Christendom, would conquer the English colonies on the Atlantic seaboard, at which happening the Maryland Catholics would have a new prestige. Our land promised to be a part of the world where all great things would be done in Our Lady's name.

Yet, as the decades went on, the prospect changed. The English took Florida from the Spanish and obliterated the Indian Commonwealth there. They took Canada from the French and closed the chief road of access to the Mississippi Valley to the French missionaries. By their conquests they spelled the end to all French and Spanish devotions to Our Lady in all land east of the Mississippi. As for the English devotions to Our Lady in Maryland, they were not affected by these conquests but they were dying for a different reason. In 1773 the Pope himself had suppressed the Jesuit order, and by so doing had deprived the Maryland Catholics of the possibility of receiving any more priests. Under this blow they were at last losing heart. Their prayers to the Queen of Heaven were becoming feebler and feebler.

In 1775 a prophet would have been wise in prophesying that within two generations, at the most, there would be not a single prayer to Our Lady heard anywhere in our land. It was evident that the French King and the Spanish King had lost all interest in adding any part of this land to their domain.—One could see that by the way that the French King offered Louisiana to the King of Spain in 1763, and by the way that the Spanish King accepted it only reluctantly.—It was evident too, that the French and Spanish missionaries had, except in California, ceased to have an interest in adding it to Our Lady's domain. In France any devotion to Our Lady among the book-learned had almost disappeared. The people who had their eyes on our land, and who were aggressive and enterprising and not to be balked, were the two million and more English-speaking colonists pressed into the narrow strip of our Atlantic coast-land. They were looking for new fields to till. They were about to press west. And they had, as a whole, no respect for Our Lady at all. They had inherited the idea that they were continuing a Protestant Crusade. On their way westward they would feel that they were doing something righteous in destroying any vestige of the Catholic faith in their way, whether it appeared in Indians, or in the Spanish, or the French. They would pass through New Mexico, and, though they would not massacre the Spanish Catholics there, they would treat them as not worthy to exist, and probably they would cease to exist— at least as Catholics. They would at last come to the Pacific, but before they arrived there, the Catholics of Maryland would have become suffocated by the atmosphere around them.

But this prophecy never came to pass, not wholly. It is curious how half of it came to pass, and half of it not. The English-speaking colonists did sweep over the Alleghenies, across the Mississippi, past Santa Fe to the Pacific, and most of them thought that they were on a Protestant Crusade, but they never established that Protestant empire in which Catholics could not live. In fact, no sooner had the prophecy been made, than the devotions to Our Lady began to revive in our land. All the devotions that had been in it once, and then had been lost—and this includes those of the Norse—became restored. And then when they had been restored, and were in full life, then new devotions were added to them. It was in that very year 1775 that the tide turned, and it is still in flood.

How did this come about? We, who cannot see into heaven, cannot wholly explain it. We face the happening rightly with a kind of awe. But, looking at things visible, we can detect somewhat the play of cause and effect. And it would be ungrateful not to study in wonder the sequence of events.

One thing is certain: there would never have been this turn of the tide if the devotions to Our Lady of the English-speaking Catholics had not been rekindled. And, looking at those devotions and at the English-speaking Catholics who did revive them, we might hit upon an all-too-simple explanation of how they revived. We see that the tide began to turn in 1775, and 1775 is a date familiar to us as that of the year when the status of all the English colonists began to change. A War of Independence then broke out, which led to the establishment by the English colonists of a new nation in our land. In that new nation religious toleration was allowed. Naturally therefore the English-speaking Catholics then took heart and began to pray to Our Lady once again.

But truly it required more than this political event to revive the English devotions. Indeed, the event might have had a contrary effect. The Catholics in the new nation might well have felt so proud to be citizens of this "land of liberty" that they might have lost their pride in being Catholics. They might have felt such an elation at being treated pretty much like anyone else, that they might have wanted to be treated entirely like anyone else. They might have ceased to be Catholics, or they might have chosen to continue Catholics, and yet give up their devotions to Our Lady as not essential, and as something that brought a mockery upon them. Something more than a political event was needed to enkindle the devotions to Our Lady of the English-speaking Catholics in the new nation.

That something more, that something else, was Bishop John Carroll, our first bishop. Carroll was a Marylander by birth, and, though he had been educated in France, and there become a Jesuit priest, he had remained at heart a Marylander. In his heart he had the inherited devotion of Marylanders to Our Lady, but, owing to personal experiences, he had it in an unusual intensity. When he had been informed of the impending suppression of his Order, the Jesuits, he had been praying to Our Lady at her shrine in Italy, at Loreto. He never forgot his prayers to her on that day, and, whenever again he found himself in distress, the same prayers came to his lips. Thus, when on the Feast of the Assumption in 1790 he was consecrated bishop, it was not merely in recognition of that feast but because he was in agony at the task ahead of him, that he entrusted his task to her as Queen of Heaven, and dedicated his diocese to her.

And throughout all his life as bishop, a quarter of a century, he continued to show his devotion to her. Not a man given to wearing his heart on his sleeve, and, keeping that eighteenth century reserve characteristic of many of his contemporaries, he did not show his fervor so much in exhortations as in the formal acts of a formal man. He chose her heavenly image as his seal, he prescribed that

130

the Litany of Loretto should be recited before every High Mass in his diocese. In 1805 when he laid the corner-stone of what was to be Baltimore's Cathedral he saw that its title should be that of the Assumption. When the British besieged Baltimore in 1814 he invited his faithful to pray to Our Lady for Baltimore's defense. When in the next year he lay dying, he, in spite of his reserve, confessed to those about him that, if there was anything he had done as bishop of which he was wholly glad, it was that he had entrusted his diocese to Mary, the Queen of Heaven.

It might seem that these acts of his in devotion to Our Lady might have escaped notice as simply perfunctory. But it happened that they were just what was needed to awaken devotions to her among his flock. His English-speaking Catholics recognized that he, so little given to risking any possible criticism from the Protestants about him, had dared to give her public honor, and they, who had been keeping their devotions to her more and more private, were encouraged to do likewise. And that they responded is witnessed to by various facts such as that one of his first priests, Father Gallitzin, named the Catholic settlement that he established in Western Pennsylvania, Loretto, after the Loreto dear to his bishop; and that when a group of transplanted Marylanders in Kentucky began one of the first orders of religious sisters in our country in 1812, they again used this name of Loreto, calling themselves the Sisters of Loretto at the Foot of the Cross.

It was in this very normal manner that the fading devotions to Our Lady of the Marylanders were revived, but how were the French devotions revived? How could they have been revived? The Catholic French and Catholic Indians of what was our Northwest Territory were not particularly elated at finding themselves a part of the new United States. Nor were they stirred spiritually by any words of Bishop Carroll, which they could not hear. Almost totally deprived of priests, they were not in condition to revive anything. The French devotions revived by being brought into our country again, this time by French priests arriving at our Atlantic seaports, driven across the ocean by the French Revolution.

The French Revolution was beginning at the moment when Bishop Carroll was being consecrated, and during his first years as bishop it was in full swing. No decree of the Revolutionaries specifically exiled priests from France, but they could stay there only by swearing an oath incompatible with their loyalty to the Pope, so that the better of the priests had either gone into hiding or had fled to foreign lands. The distant foreign land of the United States of North America received a score of them. Now, these better priests owed their firmness, almost invariably, to their devotion to Our Lady, which they had inherited from France of the seventeenth century, and those who came to our country were conspicuous in such devotion. A number of them belonged to that Institute, which can be called Marian, the Congregation of Saint-Sulpice, which had been founded by a Marian priest, Father Olier, in France's great Marian century. These latter priests, Sulpicians, who were chiefly dedicated to teaching candidates for the priesthood, set up a seminary, Saint Mary's, in Baltimore, our first seminary, and thus had an effect on all the rising generation of new priests, inspiring them with their French devotions to Our Lady. The other French priests spread the same devotion among the small groups of generally uninstructed Catholics which had formed in our Atlantic seaports, but also, more dramatically, carried them westward to the frontier, restoring them at last to the savages and few French of the Mississippi Valley among whom they had almost disappeared.

The English and French devotions to Our Lady, which had sprung back into life almost simultaneously, did not go on existing separately. They merged with one another and created among the Catholics in the new nation a simplicity and humility especially necessary to the Church at that time. After the War of 1812 an immigration from Europe set in, largely Catholic. The Catholics were mostly Irish and German, and they were not the well-to-do, nor the book-learned. They came with little except their *Ave Marias*. Had they found no devotions in our land into which their *Ave Marias* could fit, they might have wondered if the Catholic Church of their new home were really the Catholic Church of their old one, and might have ceased to be Catholic. But, as it was, they did, most of them, remain Catholic, and the number of Catholics in our land consequently increased enormously. It increased so much that thirty years after Archbishop Carroll's death, there were over a million Catholics in our land, and they had nearly eight hundred priests, and twenty-six bishops. The Church had so grown—owing largely to its possession of the devotions to Our Lady—that the Protestants were in consternation at its size. They rose up in fury. Protestant mobs attacked Catholic Churches throughout the nation, and even burned those of them in the usually peaceful city of Philadelphia. And other Protestants, such as were not given to mob violence, organized a political movement, known as Nativism, which aimed by legal methods to deprive Catholics of their civil rights. One can almost say that the devotions to Our Lady had brought the Catholics into a peril they had not foreseen.

It was when this peril was at its height that the Bishops of our land convened in Baltimore in 1840, in the Sixth Provincial Council. They were one and all in dread of what might impend, but what measures could they take to extricate themselves from their dilemma? Only a decline in their numbers could allay the alarm of Protestants, and placate them; and how could they, as apostles, wish for that? They were caught in a trap. An appeal to public opinion in the land, asking for justice, would probably not be heard at all. If it were heard, it would simply arouse anger.—How dared "Popish" bishops dictate to free Americans.—In their helplessness they could think of nothing else to do but to appeal to Our Lady, praising that privilege of hers, through which the most impossible things had come to pass, her Immaculate Conception. They dedicated themselves and their flock, the Church in our land, to Our Lady in her Immaculate Conception.

In so doing they were not starting a devotion unheard of in Baltimore, Philadelphia, or Saint Louis. The laity of our land were perfectly familiar with the phrase: *Immaculate Conception*. Yet the devotion did not occupy nearly as prominent a place among them as it had among the Spaniards who had come to our Southland of old. Thus in taking this step the Bishops were doing something Spanish. They were setting La Purisima in the place that the Spaniards had given her. They were adopting and reviving a Spanish devotion.

This is wondrous, but it is much more wondrous, when we realize that they did it without knowing what they were doing. Of course, they knew that they were crying

134

to Our Lady for help under a title which had by then not been defined, and concerning the definition of which there was some dispute. They knew that they were showing a loving audacity. But they had no idea that they were doing anything Spanish. They were much less aware than we are of what the Spaniards had once done in our land, and they did not in their minds associate the devotion to the Immaculate Conception with Spaniards at all. And if they had associated that devotion with those Spaniards, they would only have been deterred from adopting it, for at this time our country was at war with Mexico, and the Catholics of our country were being accused of a traitorous sympathy for the Catholic Mexicans. Nothing could have been more inopportune than even to seem to be doing anything Spanish.

Yet, whatever may have been the motives of the Bishops, the fact is that in 1846 the Spanish devotion was revived in our land by bishops sitting in Baltimore. It was revived just in time to enable the United States, which was at this moment conquering our Southwest from Mexico, to enter that territory carrying the very devotion which had originally brought the Spaniards there. It was revived just in time to give to the Catholics in the East of our land just enough of that optimism, which had once been Spanish, so that they could weather the hostility of the Nativists about them.

Nativism began to die down.—It was, indeed, the quarrel over slavery that put a temporary end to it, rather than any change of heart among the Nativists.—Smoother days for the Church seemed ahead, and the Catholics of our land now had all the devotions to Our Lady, that had ever been in their land, alive in their keeping. It seemed that they needed no more to overcome their future difficulties, when suddenly new devotions to Our Lady began to be given to them.

Whence came these devotions? They were not brought to them by missionary priests from other lands, nor by the millions of Catholic immigrants pouring into our land. They did spring from the hearts of the Catholics in our land, both the laity and the clergy, but they did not spring from nothing. They sprang from the seed scattered in their hearts by a series of papal pronouncements about Our Lady, beginning with the Bull, *Ineffabilis,* in 1854, and by a parallel series of Apparitions of Our Lady, herself, beginning with that of Lourdes in 1858. The Bull, *Ineffabilis,* published by Pope Pius IX defined the Immaculate Conception of Our Lady. The Apparition at Lourdes confirmed the same doctrine. In the hundred years since the Bull the papal pronouncements have continued. And the apparitions also have continued, of which the best known is that of Fatima in 1917.

What were these new devotions? Was there anything new revealed in these pronouncements and apparitions that necessitated new formulas for our prayers to Our Lady? The Bull, *Ineffabilis,* did not tell anything new to the Catholics of the United States in declaring that Our Lady had been immaculately conceived, for had they not recognized that already in dedicating the Church in their land to the Immaculate Conception? As for the definition of her Assumption issued by Pope Pius in 1950, was it not merely stating what had long been believed by all Christians? The apparition at Fatima gave an emphasis to Our Lady's Immaculate Heart, but our land had already heard of that in some of the teaching of the French priests who

136

came to our land in the seventeenth century. Other pronouncements made more clear the part of Our Lady as Distributrix of all Graces, and as Co-redemptrix, but had not that part been always implicitly accepted?—Do theological precisions demand new devotions?—Why not say that the pronouncements and apparitions evoked no new devotions at all; they merely quickened those inherited from the English, French and Spaniards?

We might say that, if we look merely at the changing of words in our prayers. But we would do better to look at the meaning that has been added to our prayers. The prayers to Our Lady are not really the same as they were a hundred years ago simply spoken with more fervor. The effect of the apparitions and pronouncements has been a transforming one. To measure that transformation we have only to imagine how different now all our prayers to her would be—our simplest *Ave Marias,* if we had not Lourdes before our eyes, and the remembrance in our mind that the present Holy Father has dedicated the world to Our Lady's Immaculate Heart. The whole position of Our Lady in regard to our final salvation and our life in this world has been enhanced.

These new devotions did not come to us all at once. They came to us gradually as our needs grew. First they gave us a strength in passing through our Civil War. Then they helped us in the tremendous task of assimilating the hordes of immigrants that arrived in our country in the half century that followed that war—the greatest displacement of population then known in human history. They prepared the Church in our land to graduate from its missionary status and come of age. They gave us our courage in establishing a Catholic system of education.

They were the incentive to stir us to the sending out of missionaries to pagan lands, chiefly through the founding of our Society of Foreign Missions, named after Mary, Maryknoll. More lately, they have become our chief weapon in facing, together with all of Christendom, secularism, especially in its most aggressive form, Communism. By them we have come to see our part in the impending battle between Our Lady's heel and Satan. She is our hope for peace, our sole hope, our *Regina Pacis*.

From this account, which I have been giving of devotions to Our Lady in our land, it might seem that I were boasting that the land were richer in devotions to her than any other land. How could it not seem so, when I have been using words that are usually used in regard to the acquisition of an earthly fortune? I have reported that no treasure has been lost in a thousand years, and that new treasure has always been coming in. But really I am making no such boast. Chiefly what I have been saying amounts to no more than this: if Catholics in our land have ever been presented with difficult tasks they have been given devotions to Our Lady wherewith to perform them, and they have never accomplished anything notable except in dedication to her. As for our present devotions, they are not so rich as to make us proud but they are rich enough to make us grateful.

It does us no harm to remind ourselves that we have these devotions, for there are those who tell us that we do not have them at all, or that, if we do have them, they are empty. It is easy to miss any sign that they exist. For instance, a European traveler would be looking for the innumerable shrines to Our Lady in field and hill, that still dot the European landscape, and he would be disappointed.

138

Yet there are other signs of our devotions and of the reality of them. There is the unexpected phenomenon of the recent sudden increase in contemplative vocations. Then here and there, there is that happy mingling of the sacred and profane which was characteristic of men who had Mary in their mind during the Middle Ages or who have her in mind now. An example of it that might startle a traveler would be the sight of Catholic students playing their very modern football not only for Notre Dame University, but for Notre Dame, Our Lady. And, finally, we Catholics in this land today have been able to keep alive and intact that Christian optimism, which cannot exist at all unless God's creation, all of it, is seen as beautiful because of its beautiful apex, Our Lady.

And we do have shrines, even if an ordinary traveler might not be termed blind or negligent in not seeing them. Some of them are even picturesque, for they are so ancient that they might appear to be ancient even to a European. There is that of Nuestra Señora de La Leche at Saint Augustine, Florida, the cult of which began soon after the Spaniards made their settlement there in 1565, but which we still honor and embellish, though the Spaniards have gone. There is that of Our Lady as La Conquistadora at Santa Fe, New Mexico, the cult of which began in 1693, and which is still honored by the Spaniards of that region, and also by those who have come to live among them. And, less antique, there is the shrine of Our Lady of Prompt Succor at New Orleans. It was founded by French nuns, Ursulines, in 1810 but was soon incorporated into our own national history; for on the eve of the Battle of New Orleans in 1815 the Catholics of the city gathered around it to pray for the victory of Andrew

Jackson, and after the victory, Jackson visited it himself twice to give thanks. And then in recent times we have builded our modern shrines. True, they are not generally in hill and valley, charming the landscape as are those of Europe, for the Catholics in such places are lacking, but they are in the populous, not always sightly, suburbs of our cities among the multitudinous Catholic poor. One of them is the Basilica of Our Lady of Perpetual Help in Boston, Massachusetts, founded in 1870. Another is the National Shrine of Our Lady of Victory in Lackawanna, New York, founded in 1926. And then, different in origin, and belonging to our nation as a whole, there is the Shrine of the Immaculate Conception at Washington, D.C., of which the cornerstone was laid in 1920, and which is not yet completed. Huge it will be, but it can serve as a wayside shrine for us all, and especially or immediately for the scholars of the Catholic University on the grounds of which it is being erected.

And also we have a shrine of world-wide fame which is ours though not on our soil, that of Our Lady of Guadalupe in Mexico, near to Mexico City. I call it ours not merely because it stands in our New World, but because Our Lady, in appearing there to an Indian, in 1539, was showing her solicitude not only for Indians of that vicinity at that time, nor for all Indians in the New World at any time, but for all the children of the New World at any time; and the New World includes our land. The present Holy Father, Pope Pius XII, reminded us of this when, through a representative of his at that shrine in 1945, he told us that Our Lady of Guadalupe was the hope for all the Americas, the hope for all who live in the Americas.

Our Lady of Guadalupe pray for us.

Our Lady and the
University of Notre Dame

Eugene P. Burke, C.S.C.
UNIVERSITY OF NOTRE DAME

Our Lady and the University of Notre Dame

From its very inception, Notre Dame University has been a shrine dedicated to The Mother of God. When in 1842 Father Edward Sorin and his little band of religious came to what was then a snowy waste, it was known to the few inhabitants of South Bend as Lac Sainte-Marie. This name was given it by the early missionaries who had preached the Gospel to the Indians, so it was natural that Father Sorin should call the University he had agreed to establish as a condition of his receiving this land, the University of Notre Dame. But this was only one reason; a more compelling one was his ardent devotion to the Mother of God which he had cherished from his childhood. This was the source of his extraordinary courage—what looked sometimes like reckless daring; but it was really his indomitable faith in Mary. He seemed to say, "I can do all things in her who guides and protects me." And indeed it was supernatural courage. He had agreed to establish in this wilderness a Catholic university. But with what? With empty hands and empty pockets, but with an unshakeable faith that she under whose patronage he had begun this work would somehow and in her own time accomplish it.

As he stood by Saint Mary's Lake on his first visit to Notre Dame, his faith in Mary seemed to cast up before him a picture of the future which Mary would make a reality. There arose stately buildings, college classrooms, laboratories for the pursuit of science, residence halls for students who would come from all parts of America, and perhaps from beyond the seas which washed her shores. He saw distinguished professors, members of his own community and scholars from many nations bringing their culture and professional knowledge to the youth of America. And under the influence of that faith-inspired picture he wrote that he dedicated them all to the Mother of God; and from that moment he never feared, he never faltered, he never doubted that that picture would be filled in with every detail. He would not live, he knew, to see its greatest development; but it could not surpass the outlines of his dream.

He set himself to work at once to build his school. First with brick and mortar, he set up a very primitive first college building which housed the little faculty and student body, and the workmen who wielded the hammer and chisel and trowel. Then there were shops to be built, and a barn for his few horses; but he was ready by the next year to begin his work of education. As his little colony grew he never for a moment was unconscious that the Lady of his heart was directing the work, and at each stage of its progress, he seemed to autograph it with some shrine or other to the Lady of the Lakes. He erected a

144

modest chapel which he named the Portiuncula chapel in honor of our Lady of the Angels, and obtained the special indulgence attached to the chapel erected by Saint Francis of Assisi. Later there was built a small shrine of the Assumption, containing a "tomb" of the Blessed Virgin, which in season was filled with cut flowers from the nearby fields. When he was able to build a separate church he established the Confraternity of the Holy Rosary and from that day on, every first Sunday of the month, the religious marched in procession, chanting the *Ave Maris Stella* and closing with the recitation of the Rosary and Benediction. This church was the most impressive building on the campus. He obtained the services of Gregori, a noted Italian artist to adorn it with paintings, and here again, he depicted the life and virtues of the Mother of God. From Le Mans, France he brought the stained glass windows in almost everyone of which you will find, in large or small proportions, the image of Mary. Two of the chapels adjoining the sanctuary have windows which are devoted exclusively to the life story of Our Lady.

In 1865 when the close of the Civil War brought a considerable increase to his religious community, he established the *Ave Maria,* a weekly family magazine devoted to the honor of the Blessed Virgin. At that time it was one of the very few Catholic magazines in this country, and became regular reading for thousands of American families. Cardinal Hayes in an address at the dedication of the Notre Dame Law building said, "I was brought up on the *Ave Maria.*" For many years the type was set by the sisters of Holy Cross, and the press work done by the brothers.

The month of May was from a very early day celebrated

with special devotions. On the eve of the opening day, the student body, the religious and lay faculty residing on the campus, gathered in the church where usually the President of the University addressed the congregation; then there followed a procession around the church while all joined in singing hymns to Mary, the ceremony closing with Benediction of the Blessed Sacrament. On each following Wednesday there was a sermon on some virtue of Our Lady, and Benediction of the Blessed Sacrament. All the students were required to attend these devotions which continued until the student body grew so large that they could not fit in the chapel at one time. The Most Reverend John O'Hara, C.S.C. who, as Prefect of Religion, promoted frequent Communion among the students until Notre Dame was known through the country as the "City of the Blessed Sacrament," joined with this practice, devotion to the Blessed Virgin.

In the year 1896, the Reverend Thomas Carroll, rector of Saint Joseph's church, Oil City, Penna., who had lived for some time in Holy Cross Seminary at Notre Dame, had erected, a few hundred yards east of Saint Mary's Lake, a replica of the grotto of Lourdes. Under the direction of Archbishop O'Hara, the grotto became a spiritual rendezvous for the student body. They could be found there in little knots on their way to and from class, and frequently in the spring and early summer fairly large groups visited the grotto before retiring for the night. At the suggestion of the students, the daily adoration which marked the month of October and the Lenten season, was extended to the month of May also; and, in the evening, as many as a thousand to fifteen hundred gathered at the

146

foot of the statue of Our Lady of Lourdes to sing a few hymns and recite the *Salve Regina*. In the summer months, the annual laymen's retreat, and the various congresses and institutes which meet at the university, close their meeting with a procession of the Blessed Sacrament starting from the church and ending with Benediction and frequently a sermon at the grotto of Our Lady.

But perhaps, the best and most distinctive symbol of Notre Dame's devotion to the Mother of God is the large statue of Mary atop the golden dome of the present administration building. For three quarters of a century it has looked down upon the activities of the campus, and has been an inspiration and source of encouragement to thousands of students and professors who have lifted their eyes heavenward as they passed over the network of pathways on the campus.

The new college building erected in 1865 was crowned with a small dome and statue of the Mother of God, a new autograph of Notre Dame's faith in Mary. It was a great source of pride to the Founder, and when in 1879 a devastating fire laid this building in ashes, Father Sorin gathered his Community in the main chapel and said to them, "If the fire had taken everything, I would begin anew." Begin he did, and by September of the same year, the present administration building was ready for occupancy, a feat of building that would be impossible today. The center of the building was again a dome which was to be based on solid brickwork built from the ground up. But money was scarce, and the University council, with great prudence, demurred at erecting the dome at this time. To Father Sorin this seemed a lack of faith in the

Lady of his heart, and he was obstinate. He went over to Saint Mary's College and remained there, refusing to sign other bills, until the council had given its consent for the dome and the statue of Mary. They gave in, and the work began, Father Sorin never doubting that somehow, somewhere he would raise the money. When the dome was nearing completion, the students of Saint Mary's asked that they might be allowed to present the statue, to which request Father Sorin enthusiastically acceded. It was an answer to his trust in Mary. The students, too, selected it—a replica of the statue of the Immaculate Conception erected by Pope Pius IX in the Piazza di Spagna in Rome to commemorate the promulgation of the dogma. That statue has been the image that thousands of students have carried lovingly in their memories into the trenches of Europe and the fox holes of Okinawa. They have written back to priests at the university that when the going was difficult they have often cast their eyes across the oceans to the Lady on the Dome and found courage and comfort in the memory.

Some twenty years ago G.K. Chesterton gave a series of lectures at the university and had opportunity to observe the students and their life on the campus. Before he returned to England he recorded his impressions in a poem, the outstanding feature of which is the Lady on the Dome and her influence on the university's life. He contrasted a great golden statue on the house of Nero looking down upon the Roman arena at the death and slaughter of the slaves who had no hope but death, with the golden image of Mary looking down upon the campus of Notre Dame. Here, too, young men engaged in combat: in games of sport and in the intellectual jousts of the class-room. But while the

Roman slaves greeted the emperor with the slogan, "We about to die, salute thee," the legions of Mary cry, "We about to live, salute thee." Not slaves, these men, but free of all things, under the law of the Gospel:

> "Queen of Death and Life undying
> Those about to live salute thee;
> Not the crawlers with the cattle; looking deathward
>   with the swine,
> But the shout upon the mountains
> Of the men that live forever
> Who are free of all things living but a Child; and He
>   is thine."

This poem has caught the true spirit of Notre Dame, that intangible something which the newspapers have never been able to explain, because they never understood that Notre Dame, its spirit and life, were but the reflection of devotion to the Lady on the Dome.

And so Father Sorin's dream in the course of a hundred years has come to reality: new buildings, new and varied colleges and courses, but the same spirit and devotion to the Mother of God which marked its beginning, and has overshadowed it with blessing through all its years. And its spirit has gone even beyond the confines of this campus. Father Patrick Peyton, fired with the spirit that burns so brightly in this shrine of Mary, lighted here the torch of his Family Rosary Crusade which he has carried across the world. In Canada, the United States, Australia, England and Ireland, Spain and India and Burma and Pakistan, hundreds of thousands of people have gathered to pledge themselves to the recitation of the family rosary, and to do penance in response to the word of our Lady of

Fatima. How far this little candle, lighted in the snowy wastes of Lac Ste.-Marie over a hundred years ago, throws its light! Mary and the University of Notre Dame, its progress and whatever triumphs it may achieve, will forever be identified as they have been beautifully identified in the Alma Mater song composed by a former president, the Reverend Charles O'Donnell, C.S.C.:

> Notre Dame, our Mother,
> Tender, strong and true,
> Proudly in the heavens
> Gleams thy gold and blue.
> Glory's mantle cloaks thee,
> Golden is thy fame,
> And our hearts forever
> Praise thee, Notre Dame.
> And our hearts forever
> Love thee, Notre Dame.

DATE DUE

GAYLORD — PRINTED IN U.S.A.